THE BATTLE FOR THE SOUL

THE BATTLE
FOR THE SOUL

Aspects of Religious Conversion

by
OWEN BRANDON

Philadelphia
THE WESTMINSTER PRESS

Library of Congress Catalog Card No. 60-7327

Typeset in Great Britain
Printed in the United States of America

CONTENTS

▼

FOREWORD

THE very considerable value of this book consists mainly in two things:

Firstly, it is the work of one who has for many years been engaged both in a pastoral–evangelistic ministry and in specialised research in the psychology of religious experience and in parallel fields of study.

Secondly, it places the work of evangelism firmly in the context of the day-to-day life of the Church. As such it will, I am sure, be of great help to those whose work is, in some specialist way, the work of evangelism, and also to those who see that all Church work should be conducted with a view to the seizing of the evangelistic opportunities which constantly present themselves to those who have eyes to recognise them.

I hope that we shall have from the pen of the Reverend Owen Brandon further works in which he puts at our disposal the results of his continuing research.

DONALD BRADFORD

INTRODUCTION

THE appearance in quick succession of three important books on the subject of religious conversion has prompted me to prepare for publication material which has been accumulating over a number of years. The Archbishop of Cape Town's little book, *This is Conversion*,[1] is written from the practical point of view; Dr. Erik Routley's work, *The Gift of Conversion*,[2] is a theological study written with deep spiritual insight; and *Battle for the Mind*,[3] by Dr. William Sargant, is written from the physiological point of view, and contributes scientific data which every serious student of the subject and every evangelist and pastor ought to ponder.

Two other books of importance, on a related subject, also call for special mention. These are: *The Whole Gospel for the Whole World*,[4] by the Reverend Alan Walker, and *What is Evangelism?* [5] by the Reverend Douglas Webster. Mr. Walker examines past and present methods of evangelism, and indicates what he believes to be necessary in the way of message and method for present-day evangelism. Mr. Webster's study is both theoretical and practical. He says:

[1] *This is Conversion*, by Joost de Blank, Archbishop of Cape Town. London: Hodder & Stoughton Ltd., 1957.
[2] *The Gift of Conversion*, by Erik Routley. London: Lutterworth Press, 1957.
[3] *Battle for the Mind: A Physiology of Conversion and Brain-Washing*, by William Sargant. London: Heinemann, 1957.
[4] *The Whole Gospel for the Whole World*, by Alan Walker. London: Marshall, Morgan & Scott, 1958.
[5] *What is Evangelism?* by Douglas Webster. London: Highway Press, 1959.

'I have concentrated rather on the *meaning* of evangelism and, on some of the questions, theological and otherwise, which it raises to-day both at home and overseas." One of his aims is "to show that evangelism in to-day's world is not easy and that all who are wanting to engage in evangelism must be prepared to do some hard thinking."

The present work is intended as a psychological and pastoral study. Its material derives from three main sources: From long personal experience in evangelistic and pastoral work; from some acquaintance with the literature of revival; and from years of specialised study and research in the field of the psychology of religious belief and experience. Its purpose is to report the writer's main findings in the study of religious conversion. Some of the facts herein recorded are already well known, others are less well known, and some have emerged as new insights — new, at least, to the writer — as a result of analytical study and reflection.

This is intended to be a serious study of a somewhat controversial subject. Its style, therefore, is analytical, and its language is that of the lecture-room rather than that of the pulpit. This is deliberate, and the serious reader will no doubt appreciate the reasons for it. There is no attempt here to explain away conversion, but the attempt is made seriously to understand it. For the Christian believer there is something mysterious and supernatural about religious conversion, but that is something which cannot be scientifically studied: it just has to be accepted, and many earnest believers are willing simply to accept it. In the present work, however, attention is focused upon the observable phenomena. This is necessary if its findings are to claim anything like scientific validity, hence the emphasis on human facts and factors.

Perhaps a word in reference to terminology would be helpful here. In the pages which follow I speak of *the subject*. I mean, of course, the person experiencing conversion. It is the term normally used in reports on investigation research projects, and is a useful term here, for it covers every type of convert — man, woman, or child. I also frequently use the word *evangelist*. This, again, is intended as a general term. As used here it means not only the professional evangelist as such, but also the pastor or priest, the parent, the Sunday School teacher, the Bible Class leader — anyone, in fact, who is engaged in any form of religious propaganda aimed at winning others to allegiance to Christ. Where the professional evangelist alone is in mind, this is clearly indicated.

It is notoriously difficult for a new writer to visualise who his readers will be; but this book is addressed mainly to clergy and ministers and to professional evangelists, and I hope that it may be of some value to lay helpers many of whom spend a great deal of time in voluntary Church work with a view to communicating the Gospel to their contemporaries. I should like, also, to think that it might be read by some who are engaged professionally in the sphere of psychology, for they must often have to deal with problems that are associated in some way with religious "crisis" experience; and the more insight they have into such experience the better.

This book is an expansion of an article which appeared in *The Church Quarterly Review*, July–September, 1958, and I wish to express my sincere thanks to the Editor of that journal, the Right Reverend and Right Honourable J. W. C. Wand, K.C.V.O., P.C., D.D., for permission to use the material of that article in this way. I also desire to place on record my gratitude to the Right Reverend Dr. F. D. Coggan, Lord Bishop of Bradford, for writing the Foreword to this book, and also for his interest, support, and encouragement in the research work which I have done and am still doing. Also, I wish to thank the Reverend F. J. Taylor, Principal of Wycliffe Hall, Oxford, and the Reverend Dr. Erik Routley for having read the first draft of this book in typescript and for valuable suggestions in regard to it.

My purpose in publishing these findings is not to attempt an answer to all the questions, but rather to raise the most important questions for pastoral practice and to direct the reader's attention to those other works where these questions are to some extent dealt with. In this connection I acknowledge with gratitude the permission to cite or to quote from particular works from the following authors and publishers: Messrs. George Allen & Unwin, Ltd.; the Editor of the *British Weekly*; Messrs. James Clarke & Co., Ltd.; the Editor of *The Ecumenical Review*; the Edinburgh University Press; the Epworth Press; the Editor of the *Evening Standard*; Messrs. John Farquharson Ltd.; the Reverend Canon Bryan S. W. Green; Messrs. William Heinemann Ltd.; The Highway Press; Messrs. Hodder & Stoughton Ltd.; The Inter-Varsity Fellowship Press; the Reverend Dr. D. Martyn Lloyd-Jones; Messrs. Longmans Green & Co., Ltd; The Lutterworth Press; the Macmillan Company of New York; Messrs. Marshall, Morgan & Scott Ltd.; the Right Reverend Stephen C. Neill, D.D.; Messrs. James Nisbet & Co., Ltd.; the Reverend Cecil Northcott; Messrs. Oliphant, Ltd.; the Reverend Dr. Erik Routley; Dr. William Sargant; the Editors of *The Scottish Journal of Theology*; the Reverend Douglas Webster; and the Reverend Canon Theodore O. Wedel, Ph.D., S.T.D.

It is right, also, that I should express my sense of indebtedness to all those who have in any way contributed to the making of this little book by providing me with so much material from their own experience of the Christian life. I am grateful to be able to draw upon so much intimate material. I am thankful to have shared the confidence of so many people over so many years. This has been a sacred experience for me; and I trust that something of that sense of sacredness will be preserved in its retelling.

The title of this book — *The Battle for the Soul* — was suggested by Mr. Leonard Cutts to whom I am indebted for much help in preparing the work for publication. Dr. William Sargant has rightly described modern propaganda as a battle for the mind. In this book we are concerned with that special type of religious propaganda which we generally call *evangelism*, and this, in one aspect at least, can be seen as a battle for the soul. Surely this idea was present in the old-time expression "soul-winning". There is a verse in the Book of Proverbs (Chapter 11, verse 30) which reads, in the Authorised Version, "He that winneth souls is wise." The Revised Version has changed the order of the words to read, "He that is wise winneth souls." Whichever way the text is read, two ideas are plain — first, that souls have to be "won"; and second, that the battle is to the wise. It is to the wise that this book is addressed.

Chapter One

FACTS ABOUT CONVERSION

THE MEANING OF CONVERSION

RELIGIOUS CONVERSION

THE AGE OF CONVERSION

TYPES OF CONVERSION

CONVERSION AND THE INDIVIDUAL

FACTS ABOUT CONVERSION

The Meaning of Conversion

Conversion is a word with a simple definition but with a wide connotation. Basically, it means simply *a turning round*, hence *change*. Dictionary definitions include such terms as: Turning, transposition, inversion, transmutation, change.

In the language of everyday conversation, the word is used with a variety of meanings or shades of meaning, some trivial, some more profound. Perhaps we can simplify the matter by reducing the basic ideas to three, namely: Adjustment, change, integration and commitment. Thus, we speak of a convertible settee — that is, a couch so constructed that its parts can be reassembled to form a bed; or a convertible motor car — that is, one that can be made to serve as an open or as a saloon car, by the adjustment of its hood. We speak of a person's being converted (that is, his changing his opinions) to this or that political view-point; or of the housewife's being converted to this or that brand of soap-powder. When the politician remarks that he is speaking to the converted, he means that he regards his audience as a group of informed and enlightened folk who are already committed to his way of thinking. And when a man professes to be converted in the religious sense, it implies that he is committed, as deeply and as fully as it is possible for anyone to be committed, to a religious way of life.

It is usual to speak of a person's *being converted*; though, literally, the word conversion has an active rather than a passive flavour. It implies an action performed by the subject, not an operation performed on him. The political disciple converts to, rather than is converted by, a new political creed; and the housewife converts, or changes, to a new brand of soap-powder. Dr. Routley [1] suggests the legal term *fraudulent conversion* as illustrating the point. It is the individual who converts fraudulently.

This is an important point, for it places the emphasis where it should be placed when we come to study religious conversion. What we shall study, then, is something done by the subject, though the change is sometimes so radical and so far-reaching that, in recounting it, the subject is apt to emphasize what he experienced rather than what he did. And this emphasis can be misleading.

Now, conversion, in the broad sense in which we have just been discussing it, is a natural phenomenon, a fact of normal human experience. The phenomenon of change, even of fundamental change involving complete reorientation of moral outlook and behaviour, is not necessarily a religious phenomenon. Such changes occur in everyday life, and have been noted in the literature of modern psychology.

Dr. Eric S. Waterhouse [2] says: "It is recognised that sudden and lasting change of habit and thought is not peculiar to religious conversion. For example, a man I know, an express engine driver, told me he smoked half a pound of tobacco a week for many years, buying it every Saturday at the same shop. One Friday he found he had exhausted his allowance and called for an extra ounce to carry him on to the next day. 'What?' exclaimed the girl who served him. 'You want more than your half-pound? You ought to be ashamed of yourself!' The man replied at once, 'I am, and I will give up smoking.' The assistant took this as a joke, but he left the shop and laid aside his pipe. I asked him why he did so, and he simply said that if a tobacconist's assistant

[1] In a private communication.
[2] *Psychology and Pastoral Work*, by Eric S. Waterhouse. London: Hodder & Stoughton Ltd., 1939, pp. 136-7.

thought he ought to be ashamed of himself, it was time to drop the habit. I asked him if he had a great struggle or any relapse. He replied that he had not, but that when his mates chaffed him about being afraid to smoke now, he smoked a pipe in their presence and then again gave up the habit. He added that he had done the same since to prove that he was absolutely free to smoke or refrain as he thought best." Dr. Waterhouse goes on to say: "It is, of course, almost certain that the girl's remark was just the last touch that decided an unconscious struggle in his own mind, but no religious or moral factor was involved."

If one were to attempt a definition of conversion in its broad sense, as a fact of human experience, I think it would run something like this: Conversion means an individual's response to stimulus and suggestion in respect of any particular orientation of mental attitude and/or of behaviour.

The chief operative factors in any conversion — religious or otherwise, trivial or profound — appear to be: (1) *The stimulus, or conditioning process.* The subject must be aware of the existence of that towards which he turns, and must be convinced of the possibility of benefit to be derived from turning towards it. In this sense he must be, to some extent, prepared for the change. In the case of the political disciple, he must know something about his party's policy before he can be truly converted to it — that is, before he can really make it his own. And in the case of the housewife, she must have heard about the new soap-powder: the stimulus or conditioning factor may have been an advertisement, or advertisements, in a newspaper or on a television programme. (2) *The subject's response.* There can be no conversion unless the subject acts. The subject must turn, or change, or adjust himself to the object or idea towards which he converts or turns. (3) *The establishment of the chosen end, or the integration of the subject with that towards which he turns.* The political follower is not converted to the system of politics which appeals to him until he makes it his own; and the housewife can hardly be said to be converted to the soap-powder unless she uses it habitually.

These factors — the conditioning process, the personal response, and the process of integration — are fundamental to our theme, and will be taken up again at different points in our discussion. They are the very warp and woof of our subject.

Religious Conversion

In this book we are concerned with conversion in its religious setting; and from now on, when we refer to conversion, we shall have religious conversion in mind. Perhaps the best formal definition of religious conversion is that given by Professor William James over fifty years ago:

"To be converted, to be regenerated, to receive grace, to experience religion, to gain an assurance, are so many phrases which denote the process, gradual or sudden, by which a self hitherto divided, and consciously wrong, inferior and unhappy, becomes unified, and consciously right, superior and happy, in consequence of its firmer hold upon religious realities." [1]

If there is one word in this definition that might be questioned in the light of more recent research, it would be the word "consciously". It is now known that many of the antecedent influences leading to conversion are largely unconscious; and in many persons the conversion process itself is an unconscious process. More will be said of this later. For the present, William James' definition is acceptable in general terms.

William James himself described one aspect of the process of conversion as the transference of an idea from the margin to the focus of the mind. He says: "To say that a man is

[1] *The Varieties of Religious Experience*, by William James. London: Longmans, Green & Co. Ltd., 1947 edition, p. 186.

'converted' means, in these terms, that religious ideas, previously peripheral in his consciousness, now take a central place, and that religious aims form the habitual centre of his energy." [1]

Dr. G. A. Coe, another early pioneer in the psychological study of religion, described conversion in terms of *the coming-to-be of a self*. "Conversion," he wrote, "is a step in the creation of a self — the actual coming-to-be of a self. The language of the parable of the Prodigal Son, 'he came to himself', is scientifically accurate. In conversion the pronoun 'my' acquires meaning that it did not have before; mere drifting, mere impulse, are checked; my conduct and attitudes attach to me more consciously; I stand out in a new way, judging myself and my world, and giving loyalty of articulate purpose to the cause with which I identify myself." [2]

Dr. A. C. Underwood illustrates conversion in terms of complex-formation, or sentiment-formation. Describing St. Paul's conversion, he says: "In brief, what took place was a sudden irruption into consciousness of a complex which had been thrust into the unconscious by repression. Before he became acquainted with the Christian faith, the dominating complex in the mind of Paul was what we may call a Pharisee-complex. His Pharisaic zeal is evidence of this. From the first day that he heard of the Christian faith what we may call a Christian-complex began to develop. All that he subsequently heard of the Christian faith only served to further its growth and to make it more closely knit. Since this Christian-complex was in antagonism to his cherished beliefs, a painful conflict was set up, during which the offending Christian-complex was repressed — that is, unwittingly separated from the rest of the mind and driven into

[1] *Varieties of Religious Experience*, p. 193.
[2] *The Psychology of Religion*, by G. A. Coe. Chicago: University of Chicago Press, 1916, p. 171.

the unconscious. Repression, so far from destroying the complex, enhanced its potential energy by cutting it off from the rest of the mind. This energy manifested itself in further feverish persecution of the Christians. In a state of tension, the apostle journeyed to Damascus, and on the way thither the power of the Pharisee-complex to resist the Christian-complex reached its limits. An explosive change took place in which the Christian-complex rose from its burial in the unconscious and became the dominant factor in the conscious life of Paul." [1]

Dr. Erik Routley defines conversion in terms of *being* and of *freedom*. The Gospel is a call to men to STOP; to TURN; to ATTEND. "Primarily 'conversion' in Biblical thought means stopping, turning, attending. Its consequence is an experience of freedom and light . . . Conversion is primarily a matter of being . . . Conversion produces a real man, more himself than he could be in the unregenerate state." [2]

Dr. William Sargant has brought to light the physiological factors involved in conversion, and sees it as a process of *conditioning — crisis — breakdown — reorientation*.[3]

The Archbishop of Cape Town uses the illustration of a spectator who is transformed into an actor. In Church he has for years witnessed the performance of the religious drama in the chancel; then one day something happens. His isolation is broken down; the drama reaches out to embrace him in its action; he identifies himself with it; he feels himself to be at one with God and with the worshipping family of God. He has been *converted*. And henceforth he becomes an active participator in the life of the Church in which once he was but an onlooker.[4]

My own brother, the Reverend Alan N. Brandon, used the

[1] *Conversion: Christian and Non-Christian*, by A. C. Underwood. London: George Allen & Unwin Ltd., 1925, p. 178.
[2] *The Gift of Conversion*, p. 138.
[3] *Battle for the Mind*.
[4] *This is Conversion*, pp. 16–17.

most homely illustration of all. He was serving in the Army, and one day the conversation in the billet turned to the subject of religion. In the course of the conversation one of the men said to my brother: "You are different from us, you are converted." My brother asked: "What do you mean by conversion?" No one seemed to know, so they asked my brother for a definition of conversion. Instead of embarking upon a theological exposition, my brother turned to a member of the group and said: "G——, next week you are going home on leave. We understand that you are going to marry D——. There was a time when you did not know D——. But one day you met her, and from that day you knew at least of her existence. Then, either gradually or suddenly, you realised that there was something in D—— that was not in any other girl. You fell in love with her, and since then you have come to know her better: you have dedicated yourself to her; you are to be united with her, and you would live and die for her. Is that right?" G—— answered: "You are quite right." And my brother said: "Well, that is what I mean by conversion"; and then went on to show that when men come to see in Christ that "something" which marks him off from all other men, that is the beginning of a conversion which leads to self-giving and dedication and service.

Now all these are accurate descriptions of what occurs when one individual or another is "converted". And all are needed for a full understanding of the matter. The more one studies the phenomena of conversion, the clearer it becomes that no two conversions are alike. The very variety of the definitions and of the illustrations employed, is evidence of the complexity of the matter. It is true to say that there are as many types of conversion as there are individual converts, and we need many illustrations to describe them. For some individuals, conversion is essentially a re-centring of life's dominant interests; for some, it is the acceptance of a new master-sentiment; for some, a re-birth; for some, the discovery of the way of release; for some, a response to external pressures; for some, a process of internalisation, a personal identification with ideas which have long been familiar (but external) to them, and which now reach out to embrace them; for some, conversion is essentially the committing of themselves to a new love. And in any particular case, several such elements may blend to produce a complex form of the experience.

The Age of Conversion

Conversions occur at all ages, but the experience is characteristically a phenomenon of adolescence. A striking fact is that the vast majority of conversions appear to take place before the age of twenty-two years. This was noted by E. D. Starbuck [1] over half a century ago, and has been confirmed by a number of independent observers from time to time. In a recent survey of 700 cases of conversion (350 males and 350 females), it was found that: 253 of the subjects (or 36 per cent of the sample) were converted before reaching 15 years of age; 336 (or 48 per cent) were converted between 15 and 21 years of age; and only 111 (or 16 per cent) were converted after 21 years of age. The modal periods recorded were the years 15 and 16. The experience at Harringay, as reported by the Reverend Frank Colquhoun, [2] was similar. Mr. Colquhoun reports that approximately 35 per cent of those who came forward for counselling were men, and 65 per cent were women. "In both groups, just over half were young people under the age of 19, the largest age-group being, as one would expect, the 12–18."

This is not to imply that conversions in later life are not to

[1] *The Psychology of Religion*, by E. D. Starbuck. London: Walter Scott, 1901.

[2] *Harringay Story: The Official Record of the Billy Graham Greater London Crusade 1954*, by Frank Colquhoun. London: Hodder & Stoughton Ltd., 1955, p. 233.

be expected, or that they are not so important when they do occur. Indeed, some of the most striking conversions occur in adult life. And, as we shall show later, some conversions which begin in adolescence do not reach finality, or completion, until the subject reaches adult life. What an adolescent subject describes as his conversion may, in the long run, prove to be but the beginning of a conscious spiritual awakening, the first of a series of spiritual crises, all of which are needed to bring the work of conversion to fruition. This is one of the difficulties that must be admitted in any statistical presentation of conversion data. Not to admit the difficulty would be to beg an important question. When we list the ages at which conversions occur, what are we listing? Often only the beginnings of conversion, to be sure. Nevertheless it remains true that the majority of conversions at least *begin* during adolescence.

Another difficulty which must be mentioned here is that of assessing the various facts and factors in the conversion experience of children. This difficulty is not unique to the study of religious experience: it is a common problem in any kind of investigational research in which the circumstances of the subjects' childhood need to be known. In this instance, it must be conceded that much of the knowledge that we have accumulated in relation to childhood conversions is derived from the testimony of these same converts long after the experience has occurred. That conversions do occur in childhood — even in early childhood — cannot be denied; but they are not easily assessed. In most cases where the matter is being investigated, subjects are describing in adult life (and often in mature language) the experiences of years before; and it is possible for them, in all sincerity, and quite unconsciously, to read into their childhood experiences the ideas of later life; and, in that case, it is possible for them to deceive themselves and the investigator. On the other hand, other factors have to be considered. For example, since most adults are able to recall vividly some other experiences of childhood — often quite trivial experiences — it is reasonable to believe that they could recall the experience which in so many cases decided the whole direction of their lives. Indeed, I have often found that the memory of the conversion in childhood lives vividly in the subject's mind even in mature years. The very place, the exact time, the incidental details of the occasion, stand out clearly in the narrator's mind as he recalls the experience.

The question has been asked, whether *conversion* is an apt term for such an experience in childhood. Perhaps the word *response* would be a more accurate description of the experience, for before the period of conceptual thought and full volition is reached, the whole significance of conversion cannot be realised. It might be argued that until the whole personality — thought, feeling, and will — is consciously involved, the individual cannot be said to be truly converted. This, of course, is true; but even in childhood it is possible to make decisions, and religious decisions are often made.

Dr. Basil A. Yeaxlee [1] illustrates the growth of the religious sentiment in early childhood, and much of what he says is relevant here. In the first three years of a child's life, he lives in a world of percepts; his reaction to people and things is predominantly emotional. From three to six years of age he grows in imaginativeness; he experiences the beginnings of conceptual thinking; he is very open to suggestion, especially from those he loves. Between six and eleven he enters upon the stage of realism; he becomes matter-of-fact; he is still to some extent emotional, and is still responsive to suggestion; but he comes to acquire greater stability and independence of thought and action. The age six to eleven is an age of decisions; it is characterised by a transfer of interest from the subjective to the objective; the child becomes more

[1] *Religion and the Growing Mind*, by Basil A. Yeaxlee. London: Nisbet & Co. Ltd., 1945.

social in outlook than he has been hitherto. Typical of this age is the question, "Is it true?" The child manifests a desire to explore the realities of life. Everything at this stage is very personal; there is constant self-reference in relation to outward people and things; and there is growth, in the social sense, of a feeling of guilt. All these factors and functions of human development find an expression in the religious responses of children.

In psychological language the conversion of the adolescent may be interpreted in terms of *sublimation, transference,* and acceptance of a *style of life.* New outlets are found for active living; new loyalties are formed; and a sense of the purpose of life is achieved. Adolescence is the age of doubts and problems, hopes and visions; and at this age, conversion sometimes takes the form of turning from a life of seeming meaninglessness to one of dedication to a high and noble purpose.

Types of Conversion

It is usual to refer to two main types of conversion — sudden and gradual. However, my own pastoral experience and specialised study have led to the conclusion that there are at least four or five distinguishable "types", always remembering that in the last analysis no two conversions are altogether alike and that there is a danger in too rigid a classification.

The several types may be classified and described as:

(1) *Unconscious Conversion of the "Once-born" Type.* By this is meant that the process of spiritual integration which characterises religious conversion has been an unconscious process. The person has a living faith, but cannot recall any moment of decision; sometimes he is not able to remember a time when he did not believe. The "conversion" — if we may use the word in this context — was a process rather than a

crisis. The process of internalisation has been an unconscious process. The subject has come to accept the religious
ideas presented to him, and to make them his own, he knows
not how. As long ago as 1873, Dr. R. W. Dale described
this unconscious process of growth in personal religion. In
a series of papers in *The Congregationalist*, on the relation of
children to the Church, he wrote: "There are not a few who
can testify that 'from their childhood', they knew, not 'the
scriptures', but God Himself; they came to know Him they
cannot tell how; they knew Him just as they knew the blue
sky or their mother's love; they knew Him before they could
understand any name by which in our imperfect human
speech we have endeavoured to affirm His goodness, His
power, or His glory." [1]

There are many in our churches to-day of whom this is
true; and their experience is as valid, and their religion is as
vital to them, as those of their fellow church-members whose
"conversion" has been more spectacular. They are the *once-
born* type of Christians, of whom it has been said that they
have been children of God from their birth: they have never
left the Father's house or wandered into the far country.[2] It
is to be regretted that this type of conversion experience is
not always recognised by those who engage in evangelistic
enterprise.

(2) *Gradual Conversion*, often extending over a period of
months, or even years. The moment of decision is but the
climax of a period of preparation, partly conscious and partly
unconscious. Looking back, the subject is able to trace the
main paths by which he has been brought on his spiritual
pilgrimage, and perhaps can recall a special moment of
enlightenment, decision, or surrender. In this type of con-

[1] Quoted by George Jackson, in *The Fact of Conversion*, London:
Hodder and Stoughton Ltd., second edition, 1909, p. 102.
[2] F. W. Newman, quoted by George Jackson in *The Fact of Conversion*, p. 100.

version, the process is of greater significance than the crisis. It differs from what we have called *unconscious conversion* by the fact that the subject passes through a definite, conscious experience which is characterised by a transition from no religion, or a religion that is not vital, to a religion that is both vital and personal. I have had this type of experience described to me over and over again by subjects. Sometimes they describe it as a process of enlightenment; sometimes as the emergence of a new life, or of a new quality of life; sometimes as a change from formal to vital religion; sometimes as a process of development bringing them nearer and nearer to God until the final discovery is made by the acceptance of Christ as Lord and Saviour. But always the two essential characteristics are mentioned, namely: The gradual process, and the eventual crisis or climax.

(3) *Conversion by Stages.* This is a variant form of *gradual conversion*. From a careful sifting of the data, it emerged as a very definite type. The growth of the religious life is gradual, but in steps or stages that are often quite clearly marked. The development of the religious life is characterised by a series of crises. The subject is aware of spiritual progress at each stage of the experience, but at none of the stages, except the last, does he reach the sense of attainment or full conscious assurance. The process is largely conscious, and, in retrospect, the convert is able to recall and to describe the ways and means whereby he was led onward in his religious quest. In my own pastoral experience, I have found individuals who have experienced two, three, four and even five stages of conversion. I have found this a valuable insight for pastoral purposes. Its significance first became apparent to me in the context of day-to-day parish work, when one and another told me that they had been converted once, or twice, or more, but that "it hadn't worked" or that they were still living in a state of spiritual uncertainty. To give but one example:

A man in his early thirties came for spiritual counsel. He said that he had been converted three times, but that he was still not "there" spiritually. I asked him to recall in detail the circumstances of each of his three "conversions" one by one. He told me all that he could remember of each experience. He said that at the first experience he had hoped to find peace, but soon discovered that he had not fully done so. Several years later he attended an evangelistic meeting. After the meeting he sought the help of the evangelist. This evangelist told the subject that his first conversion was obviously not valid, and outlined what he ought to do, assuring him that this would lead to a valid conversion. The subject went through the motions of conversion again that night, to the evident satisfaction of the evangelist; but, again, soon found that he had not experienced what he had hoped. Shortly after, he came into contact with an evangelical clergyman who told him that neither of his previous experiences could have been valid, and offered to lead him into a true conversion. Again he went through the motions; but still without the experience of the finality which he sought. And here he was, in my study, in a state of great spiritual perplexity. Together we went over the history of his experience, point by point, and analysed each of his so-called conversions; and we discovered that each one had been a crisis following some kind of process, and that each of the crises had taken him one step further in his spiritual pilgrimage. So that there was no need to tell him that his previous experiences were not valid conversions; each had met a particular need, and his former spiritual counsellors had been mistaken in declaring his earlier experiences to be invalid. They had not helped him by making such pronouncements.

After dealing with a number of such cases, I determined to study them more deeply, and have come to the conclusion that they represent a definite type of religious conversion.

It is possible that, psychologically speaking, each stage represents an internalisation of religious truth at a deeper level of the unconscious life; though I think that there is room for further research here.

Meanwhile, to recognise *conversion by stages* as a definite and distinct type of conversion, might help many who are engaged in evangelistic or pastoral work, to deal with certain individuals more realistically. Instead of complicating matters by casting doubt upon their experiences, we might help them more by aiding them towards a better understanding of the route of their spiritual pilgrimage, as they see the steps by which they have come to their present stage of development.

(4) *Sudden Conversion.* Here the crisis is more prominent than the process; the process may have been subconscious or unconscious. In cases of *sudden conversion* the subject can often recall the time, place, and circumstances of the experience. *Sudden conversion* is often a revolutionary experience, changing completely long-standing habits of thought, feeling, and will. In analysing the details of a *sudden conversion* the preparatory process must not be ignored. As Dr. Eric S. Waterhouse has pointed out, a literally instantaneous conversion never occurs. It would be a psychological impossibility. There is always a certain amount of preparation, even if it is unconscious, to aid the adjustment of the mind to the new idea or orientation.[1] But often the preparatory process is not fully recognised by the convert himself, and is not apparent to the evangelist; hence the number of seemingly sudden conversions. St. Paul's was a *sudden conversion*, so was St. Augustine's — but no one would deny the reality of the preparatory process in either case. In every case of *sudden conversion* that I have studied, I have found it to be the climax of a process — sometimes a long process — of preparation.

[1] *Psychology and Pastoral Work*, by Eric S. Waterhouse. London: University of London Press, 1939, pp. 139-40.

(5) *Conversion and Reconversion.* A study of the varieties of conversion would not be complete without reference to an experience which might be termed "secondary conversion" or "re-conversion". This is a second definite experience which appears to become necessary in some cases of child-hood or adolescent conversion, in order to confirm and/or to complete the conversion. This type of experience differs from *conversion by stages* in several important points. In *conversion by stages*, the convert is aware of spiritual progress at each successive stage, but does not gain full assurance until the final stage has been reached. In *conversion and re-conversion*, there are two distinct experiences, both real, and, at the time of their occurrence, both final, in the consciousness of the subject. The first experience is vital, deeply affecting the person's life; but at a later stage of mental, physical, and spiritual growth, a second experience becomes necessary to meet the new need.

There is a sound psychological reason for this second ex-perience in many cases. Quite frequently, those who make a response in childhood or in early adolescence (probably under ideal conditions, in the environment of a secure and sheltered home-life) need a confirmatory experience in later life, to adjust their religious outlook to their adult way of life. The child who decides for Christ may make a real and sincere surrender, but that surrender cannot be more com-plete than the stage of his natural development will allow; neither can he apprehend in childhood all that is implied in the step that he takes. As he develops mentally and physically, and as he takes on some of the responsibilities of adulthood, new factors enter into his every-day life. If his religious knowledge and experience develop in proportion to his mental and physical growth, then he becomes a strong and intelligent Christian. But if, as is so often the case, his religious development fails to keep pace with his growing knowledge, his physical development, and his added responsibilities, then he finds himself in a state of tension between natural maturity and spiritual immaturity, and he is apt to judge religion in general, and his own religious experience in particular, in the light of his childhood response. (Perhaps this is why some who profess conversion in childhood lapse in later life.) During this period of tension there may be a time of "backsliding", or, at least, of spiritual barrenness; often there is intellectual doubt. He has to decide whether to renounce the decision of his childhood, or to seek an adjustment between it and his fuller life. At last the final decision is made; the response of childhood is confirmed. A renewed sense of joy is experienced; it seems almost like a second conversion.

This second experience is always very real. Quite often the phenomena of the first experience are repeated, sometimes in intensified forms. There is a sense of spiritual failure and frustration, a conviction of sin, a longing after holiness, and a fresh realisation of the power of the Gospel of Christ. Doubts and problems are resolved, and there comes into the soul a sense of reconciliation, release, and power. Theologically, this second experience is often associated with the doctrine of the Person and Work of the Holy Spirit, and with the idea of sanctification; whereas in the first conversion the emphasis was on the Person and Work of Jesus Christ as Redeemer. Psychologically, the main feature of the second experience is generally that of *surrender*, whilst *receiving* or *accepting* Christ is the characteristic feature of the first experience.

Conversion and the Individual

All the available evidence tends to emphasize the individual nature of the conversion experience. No two conversions are alike, and when conversion does occur, it is likely to follow a pattern, and to manifest itself in a form, that are characteristic of the individual as a person, and that

C

are suited to his particular needs. Thus, in accordance with the circumstances and with the personality of the subject, the conversion experience may appear to be predominantly either:

(1) *Intellectual* — the acceptance of a new idea, or a new understanding of an old idea: in this case the conversion is characterised by a process of mental enlightenment and of spiritual understanding; or

(2) *Emotional* — the birth of a new and dominating affection; the subject feels constrained by the love of God, and responds in love to God: in this case the conversion is characterised by a reorganisation of the emotional life around this new centre; or

(3) *Moral* — the confession of failure; a reorientation of the will in respect of its dominant aim for life.

Of course, in all conversions there is a blending of intellectual, emotional, and volitional elements; but these tend to manifest themselves in different ways and in different degrees in different individuals.

Chapter Two

FACTORS LEADING TO CONVERSION

PERSONAL ELEMENTS IN RELIGIOUS
CONVERSION

THE SENSE OF NEED

THE SENSE OF GUILT

THE VISION OF THE BETTER SELF

FEAR

RESPONSE TO DIVINE LOVE

DREAMS AND VISIONS

EXTERNAL PRESSURES

DOCTRINAL EMPHASIS

HUMAN EXTREMITY THE EVANGELIST'S
OPPORTUNITY

EVANGELISM THROUGH FELLOWSHIP
AND SERVICE

THE CHURCH AND EVANGELISM

FACTORS LEADING TO CONVERSION

WHEN we seek to go behind the conversion experience and ask: What are the factors in religious conversion? we are confronted by two sets of data, namely: *Internal states*, and *external pressures*. The two are so closely related in experience that it is difficult to separate them, but for the purposes of analysis it is convenient to do so. Here, without stressing the analysis unduly, we shall examine the parts of these two sets of data as they occur in our own findings.

Personal Elements in Religious Conversion

The element of self-reference becomes evident in the early stages of the study of conversion. Conversion is an intensely personal matter, a transaction between the individual and his God. The motives that prompt an individual to seek God are often mixed. Frequently, self-regarding motives, such as the longing for peace and inward satisfaction, the hope of overcoming the sense of failure and frustration, and the desire to escape the consequences of wrong-doing, are present; but so also are other-regarding motives, such as a desire to be worthy of the love of God, and a longing to serve Him and His children.

The Sense of Need

The desire for personal salvation springs generally from a realisation of personal need. Not every convert is able, in the pre-conversion stage, to delineate precisely the nature of the need he feels, but in retrospect most subjects acknowledge at least a vague, or general, sense of need to have been a factor in the conversion process. Typical statements are: "The sense of failure and frustration had been increasing in my life for at least two years prior to conversion." "I had a feeling of 'not being right' somehow." "I felt a deep sense of need." "I had a longing for peace. I knew that I was missing the way."

Such manifestations of the sense of need may, perhaps, be subsumed under the heading *negative self-feelings*. But sometimes the sense of need manifests itself in a more definite and positive dissatisfaction with one's own life. The feelings are mixed, and it is not always possible, even in an academic way, to distinguish between negative self-feeling and positive dissatisfaction with one's life; nevertheless, several definite forms of dissatisfaction are discernible in the data available, and they are worthy of note. These are: (1) A vague, but positive, sense of dissatisfaction; (2) A sense of lack of purpose in life; and (3) A sense of unworthiness. Here subjects speak of their conversion as "the end of self-seeking"; of "turning to Christ who alone could give a better, noble, and upright life"; of "coming to Christ as the One who could make me the person I desired to become." Here and there the element of *gratitude* shines through the clouds of sorrow and dissatisfaction. Says one subject: "I went to Christ with a feeling of gratitude, as Lord and Giver of all." And another: "My motive was gratitude for all He had done for me."

The Sense of Guilt

In a large number of cases a definite feeling to which we may attach the expression "the sense of guilt", or "conviction for sin", is present. Indeed, it appears to be an almost universal factor in Christian development, even if it is not always present in consciousness in the early stages of conversion. It would appear that the majority of those who consciously pass through the conversion process experience conviction of sin at some time in their Christian life, either before or during the conversion process, or at some time later. Some experience a superficial conviction at the time of conversion, and a deeper sense of conviction afterwards; some experience deep conviction at the time of conversion, and no more; some do not feel a definite sense of conviction at the time of conversion, but experience it later; few appear to experience no sense of conviction at all.

The Vision of the Better Self

Sometimes the feeling of conviction is accompanied by another element, which might be called the vision of the better self. Here the subject is concerned not so much with his badness as with his desire to be good. The emphasis is on striving rather than on failure. In such cases the subject turns to Christ as to a Friend and Helper, or a Leader and Guide, rather than as to a Saviour or Redeemer. Looking back upon their conversion, some of our subjects say: "I seem to have been drawn to Christ as a Leader; One who set a standard of conduct by His life and teaching. Not until later did I grasp anything of His atoning work." "I can only honestly say that I turned to the Lord as a Divine Leader for my life. I did not fully understand salvation and His atoning work." "My main conception of Christ at the time of my conversion was that of a Divine Leader, directing my life in the way in which He wanted me to go. Circumstances showed me definitely that if my ambitions were to be fulfilled, I should have to surrender my life to Christ's guidance."

Fear

Quite frequently the element of fear is one of the factors leading to conversion. The specific fears enumerated by subjects are many and varied, but by and large they may be classified as: Fears and anxieties in relation to personal life; and fears connected with death and the life to come. Generally speaking, fears connected with death and the life to come are characteristic of childhood and early youth, whilst fears and anxieties concerning this life are characteristic of later youth and adult life. In the imaginative days of childhood and early adolescence the typical fears are fear of death, of the life to come, of "being left behind" at the Last Day, and of not meeting parents and friends in heaven. In some cases there are dreams; sometimes sleeplessness in extreme cases, and intense fear. Fortunately such cases are rare, but they do occur.

Such fears tend to diminish with increasing years, whilst anxieties and fears concerning the present life tend to increase in late adolescence and early adult life. This, of course, is to be expected. As the child grows out of the imaginative stage, and enters upon the more responsible phase of adolescence and manhood, so his fears and anxieties attach themselves to the situations of his more mature life, such as business and family responsibilities, occupation, career. Thus, "anxiety about impending examinations", "fear and worry over the world-situation", "worry as to my choice of a career", "worries of the future and of taking my place in the community for the good of all", "anxiety over my inadequacy for my job", "fears and worries over family distress", are stated by the subjects to be conscious factors leading to their conversion.

Response to Divine Love

Perhaps it would be true to say that the element of response to divine love is present in every conversion. In one aspect, conversion is just that. But in some cases it is the main element, the subject being prompted to turn to God. or to Christ, in gratitude and love. Typical statements are: "I turned to Christ as to One who loves me"; "Gratitude provided the impulse. I felt that as He had died for me, I should live for Him"; "His love won my heart absolutely";

"I was drawn by His love for me"; "For the first time I realised that I was one of God's children, and that He loved me"; "His love was so wonderful; I felt I could hold out no longer."

Gratitude sometimes takes the form of a positive desire to dedicate oneself to a life of service. In some of the cases studied, subjects say that a desire to serve was one potent factor in leading them to Christ. Several say that a childlike desire "to serve God as a missionary", or "to be a minister", was a factor in their decision. In most of these cases, the "call" was confirmed later, and they did actually fulfil their ambition.

Dreams and Visions

Dreams play a greater part in religious conversion than is sometimes realised. In the course of years, I have gathered data which indicate that in some cases of conversion a dream or dreams made a decisive contribution either in the preparatory period prior to the actual conversion, or as a confirmatory experience shortly after it. It is difficult to categorize the dreams one has studied, but, roughly, in the order of frequency in which they have recurred, they may be categorized as: Dreams about heaven, death, and judgment; dreams in which Christ (or some other heavenly being, such as an angel or the Blessed Virgin Mary) is the central figure; dreams in which personal problems are in focus; dreams emphasizing the presence and power of evil.

The interpretation of dreams is a notoriously difficult matter; but frequently the subject is able to interpret his own dream or dreams, or with patience on the part of a counsellor he can be helped to interpret them.

Visions also accompany some conversions. Some of the visions of which one has been told are quite striking. Briefly, and roughly, they may be categorized in order of frequency as: Visions of the presence of God or of Christ; visions of the Suffering Saviour or of Christ on the Cross; symbolic projections of personal problems; visions of judgment; visions of heavenly beings, such as angels or departed loved ones; visions of the presence of evil.

An interesting fact, and a fact of great importance from the psychological point of view, is that over and over again these dreams and visions reflect the background and antecedent experiences of the subject himself. Thus, his dream or vision of Christ is "as He is portrayed by such-and-such an artist", or "like a picture in my first illustrated Bible." Dreams and visions can often be guides to the spiritual advisor who is sufficiently trained and skilful to use them.

External Pressures

In all my studies I have been impressed by the enormous influence of institutional religion in the formulation of religious attitudes in general, and in cases of conversion in particular. At the moment of writing I am engaged in an experimental research project specifically aimed at studying the effects of environment upon religious beliefs, so I shall say little here about the matter. But, without anticipating the results of further investigation, it can be clearly stated that the strongest influences leading young people to adopt a religious attitude to life are: The Christian home; Sunday School; Church attendance; and the Church Youth Group. Only after these, in spite of all the publicity that goes with them, do we find evangelistic campaigns; then come small-group methods, and other "informal" methods of evangelism, including radio broadcasts and religious films.

Doctrinal Emphasis

"Evangelistic preaching," writes Dr. William L. Northridge,[1] "has both a distinctive doctrinal basis and a dis-

[1] *Recent Psychology and Evangelistic Preaching*, by W. L. Northridge. London: Epworth Press, 1924, pp. 12–13.

tinctive aim. Its basis is evangelical truth. It assumes the
reality of sin, the need for and universality of atonement, and
the Saviourhood of Christ. It is the Cross, with all that this
implies as regards both God and man, that is the central and
vital theme of the evangelist. Moreover, evangelistic preaching has a distinctive aim. It is concerned not with the task
of imparting instruction on social, moral, or theological
problems, but rather with the salvation of men. This is its
primary aim. It is obvious that a preacher may be evangelical without being evangelistic. He may pin his faith to
evangelical doctrine, and may brilliantly expound it, without
either aiming directly at conversion or winning men for
Christ. But the converse is not possible. A preacher cannot
be evangelistic without being at the same time evangelical.
His appeal for men's salvation is based on the assumption
that men both need and can experience salvation; it is based,
that is, on evangelical doctrine."

This emphasis — on *sin, atonement, and the Saviourhood of
Christ* — is noted time and time again by subjects in describing the kind of preaching or teaching which led directly
to their conversion.

The Bible has always had a central place in evangelism,
and it still holds that place. The most successful evangelistic
preachers (and here I am thinking of professional evangelists)
appear to be, not those who rely for effect upon the moving
story and the colourful narrative, but those whose preaching
expounds the great Scriptural themes of God, sin, judgment,
redemption, and atonement; who show the Gospel of Christ
to be relevant to human needs; and whose appeal is based
on the authority of the revealed "Word" of God.

At one point in my investigations, I asked a large number
of people whether any particular passage or verse of the
Bible had been the means of their conversion, and, if so,
what that passage or verse had been. The most frequently
quoted verses were St. John 3: 16, "For God so loved the

world, that he gave his only begotten Son, that whosoever believeth in him should not perish, but have everlasting life"; and, Revelation 3 : 20, "Behold, I stand at the door and knock: if any man hear my voice, and open the door, I will come in . . ." The fact that these verses have to be divorced from their context to be given the desired meaning, and the question whether this is permissible from the exegetical point of view, are matters which do not concern us at this point. The fact is, that for a large number of people a word from the Bible, heard or read in the context of a specific felt need, does act as a directive to, or as a seal upon, their conversion. Other passages figuring rather less frequently than those just quoted, but often enough to justify mention here, are Isaiah 53; St. John 6: 37; St. John 1: 11–12; 1 John 1: 7–9; Romans 6: 23; Romans 10: 9. These are all verses which, in the context of evangelism, would tend to emphasize personal sin, the love of God, the atoning work of Christ, and the offer of salvation to men.

The sacramental aspect of the Church's life and worship must not be overlooked. Although not intended primarily as evangelistic media, experience shows that the Sacraments and other rites of the Church are, in some cases, aids to religious conversion. Sometimes conversion coincides with participation in one or other of the Church's ceremonies; in other cases, the outward ceremony and all that it involves in public profession, confirm a newly-found faith. Adult Baptism, Confirmation, and Holy Communion are named by subjects as the moments either of their conversion or of the confirmation of their conversion, the moment of personal assurance. Sacramental Confession also is named by some.

Human Extremity the Evangelist's Opportunity

Although it would be unfair for any evangelist to exploit human misfortune to propagate his own religious views, it is a fact that suffering sometimes does open the door to the

Gospel. In times of need, men and women who have hither-to appeared indifferent to religion sometimes turn to the Church for help; and where they find sympathy and under-standing, they often become susceptible to the evangelistic appeal. Times of anxiety, of bereavement, and of material loss are mentioned by some subjects as factors in their con-version. Seldom, if ever, are these the only factors, but they are contributory factors in some cases. And to-day, when there is a revival of interest in the Church's ministry of healing, an increasing number of persons are being con-verted in the process of seeking physical cure.

Evangelism through Fellowship and Service

In several striking cases of conversion I have studied, those in need were inspired and affected, not merely by the kind-ness of an individual, such as the clergyman or an individual Church member, but by the love and sympathy of the Church as a whole.

A middle-aged woman found herself in debt on the death of her husband. She was distraught and in despair. She had lived without religion, but friends at a local Mission Hall, hearing of her need, came to her rescue. She describes her conversion as "gradual, due to the kindness of these Christian friends who visited me in my distress."

When another woman of middle-age in straitened cir-cumstances returned to the Church from which she had lapsed, the whole church — clergy and people — rallied to her aid. They made her feel welcome, and gave of their substance to relieve her distress. She owes her conversion, she says, "to the love and kindness of friends at the Church."

Examples could be multiplied. This type of service is a great witness to the reality of Christian life and faith; but it presupposes a spirit of fellowship within the Church — a spirit which is all too rare. It means that there is mutual respect and trust between the minister and the members of his Church; and a spirit of fellowship which is outward-looking and which issues in service.

The Church and Evangelism

As a definition of evangelism, that given by the *Archbishops' Committee of Inquiry on the Evangelistic Work of the Church* in 1918, and adopted in the 1945 Report, *Towards the Conversion of England*, has never been surpassed: "To evangelise is so to present Christ Jesus in the power of the Holy Spirit, that men shall come to put their trust in God through Him, to accept Him as their Saviour, and serve Him as their King in the fellowship of His Church." [1]

There was a time, within living memory, when in large areas of Christian thinking evangelism was regarded as something apart from the Church's normal work — some activity outside of, or over and above, the Church's ordinary routine. In recent years the climate of thought has changed. In a statement issued before the war under the inspiration of Canon Bryan S. W. Green,[2] it was affirmed that "evangelism is not an activity at all. It is rather an attitude of mind behind all Christian activity. Evangelism is not a list of certain things done, but the spirit in which they are done. That is precisely why it cannot be organised. It is perhaps best described as an attitude of mind towards God and the world — an attitude which the Church must recover if she is to be true to her Lord, and to seize hold of the present opportunity." Since this affirmation was made, a great deal more thinking has been done on the subject of the Church's mission, and the ideas expressed in this affirmation have become the current opinions of Church leaders of all denominations.

In this connection, my own experience and research have led to two positive conclusions:

[1] Reproduced here by courtesy of the Church Information Office.
[2] *Evangelism: Some Principles and Experiments*, 1936, p. 8.

Firstly, *they emphasize the influence of religious background, and demonstrate the potent forces for evangelism that are inherent in institutional religion.* The Christian home, the Sunday School, and public worship are proved to be some of the most important factors in preparing the individual for conversion. Institutional religion forms a background of knowledge and experience against which the evangelistic appeal can be made. And evidence goes to show that the word of the Gospel tends to take root better in those who have a background of religious training than in those who have not such a background.

Secondly, they show that *contemporary evangelism is confined almost entirely to those who are already within the fold of the Church, or who have at least been nurtured in the Faith to some extent.* This throws into relief the enormous task of evangelism confronting the Church at the present time. It must be frankly admitted that contemporary evangelism is making very little impact on those outside the Church. Here and there an "outsider" is converted, but such cases are rare as yet. It will be interesting to watch the effects of the Church's present awareness of her mission on the rising generation.

Chapter Three

THE MECHANICS OF CONVERSION

THE MECHANICS OF CONVERSION

In Chapter One we brought together a number of descriptions of conversion by different writers. Now we shall turn our attention to the sheer mechanics of conversion.

The Conditioning Process

The first thing we notice is the conditioning process. The formative influences of the Christian home, and familiarity with the theological and ritual content of what we here term "institutional religion", are shown to be the most potent factors in conversion. This is a most important aspect of any study of conversion. From the physiological and psychological angles, Dr. William Sargant, in his *Battle for the Mind*, shows the similarity, so far as mental process is concerned, between psycho-analysis, political brain-washing, and religious conversion. The processes are, briefly: Conditioning — crisis — breakdown — surrender. Not everything that Dr. Sargant says will be acceptable to all evangelists, but the value of his contribution to the scientific understanding of the conversion process can be assessed only by a careful reading and weighing of his thesis.

But let me hasten to add that this is not altogether a new insight, though Dr. Sargant states it in scientific terms. In other ages, and in other contexts, the conditioning influence of institutional religion has been recognised. The study of the great revivals of religion leads to three conclusions. They are: (1) that the waves of religious revival observable at different periods of time, are really one movement in the ebb and flow of history; (2) that between the seasons of

revival, the lamps of religious devotion have been kept
burning in the hearts of an unbroken succession of faithful
men and women; and (3) that each movement of revival has
begun within the circle of the faithful remnant. In his pene-
trating analysis of the ebbs and flows of Christian history,
Professor K. S. Latourette has shown that each major re-
cession in the history of Christianity has itself produced the
conditions for a subsequent advance, *and that the continuing
factor has been the Church*.[1]

It is impossible to overstate the importance of the existence of the faithful remnant in the history of revival. Revival
has always been the fruit of faithful sowing, and the sowing
has been done by devout parents and pastors and teachers
during the bleak periods in the Church's life. St. Augustine,
reading his Bible and reflecting upon the state of his own
life; St. Francis of Assisi, kneeling before the Crucifix in the
derelict chapel — symbols of a dying Faith in a ruined
world; Martin Luther, grappling with the doctrine of Justification by Faith; John Wesley, rescued in childhood from
the burning rectory at Epworth, and ever after regarding
himself as "a brand plucked from the burning"; Charles
Finney, praying in the woods between two fallen trees; D. L.
Moody, determining to be, by the grace of God, the man
God could use. These are examples of the existence and of
the vitality of the faithful remnant.

In a reference to the American revivals of the eighteenth
and nineteenth centuries, the Reverend Albert Barnes of
New York, wrote in the year 1842: "The most powerful
revivals of religion in this country (i.e. in America) have
occurred in those places where the mass of people are best
educated, and where they are most sober in their lives, most
virtuous and industrious, and regular in their attendance on
the house of God . . . They have been the fruits of sound

[1] *The Unquenchable Light*, by K. S. Latourette. London: Eyre and
Spottiswoode, 1945, p. 25–6.

instruction, and of careful training in common schools and in Sabbath schools; they have occurred where the Gospel has been long and faithfully preached, and those who have been converted have been usually those whose minds have been most sedulously taught by the labours of the ministry; they have occurred eminently in our colleges and higher female seminaries — places far removed from mere enthusiasm, and places where God has made intellectual culture contribute to the purity and power of revivals." [1]

Commenting upon the Ulster revival of 1859, the Reverend S. M. Dill, of Ballymena (one of the centres of the revival), makes the following observation: "It is right it should be known that this movement has not come upon us so suddenly as people at a distance might suppose. There has been a gradual but perceptible improvement in the state of religion throughout this district for some years. Ministers were led to speak to the people with greater earnestness about 'the things which belong to their peace.' Attendance on the public ordinances of religion had considerably increased. Open-air preaching was extensively practised. Sabbath schools were greatly multiplied. Prayer-meetings were growing up in many districts. Sacred music, which had been much neglected, was cultivated with ardour and success. And altogether the people were in a state of preparation — a state which passed into one of earnest expectancy — when the glad news of the American revival reached our shores." [2] Constantly in his narrative, William Gibson, who makes this quotation from Dill, emphasizes the fact that those who were most affected by the revival in Ulster were those who had had early training in Christian homes and Sabbath schools.

[1] *Theory and Desirableness of Revivals*, by Albert Barnes. New York: Blackader, 1842, p. 146.
[2] Quoted by the Reverend William Gibson, in *The Year of Grace*, 1859. London: Oliphants, 1909, pp. 10-11.

The revival began in the heart of the Church before its influence was felt in the body of society.

Now all this has an important bearing upon our own immediate study, for it gives historical perspective to our contention that the conditioning process is the most potent single factor in the conversion of individuals.

The Individual Nature of the Convert's Response

Dr. G. A. Coe [1] gives four marks of conversion: "(1) The subject's very self seems to be profoundly changed. (2) This change seems not to be wrought by the subject but upon him; the control seems not to be self-control, the outcome not a result of mere growth. (3) The sphere of the change is the attitudes that constitute one's character or mode of life. But one's whole world may acquire new meaning; or there may be a sense of divine presence; or there may seem to come new insight into a doctrine or into a whole system of doctrine. (4) The change includes a sense of attaining to a higher life, or to emancipation or enlargement of the self. Not seldom there is victory over habits that brought self-condemnation. Now and then there is recovery from moral degradation and helplessness."

Dr. Coe proceeds to enumerate four "structural aspects" of conversion, thus:

First, we find traces of mental reproduction of the individual's own earlier experiences. "The ideational factors are predominantly reproductions from antecedent experiences of the convert himself. His notion of the 'higher' life has been formed under the influence of standards present in his environment. He is converted *to* something, the idea of which he has already met, as at home, or in Sunday School, or in preaching, or in his reading and reflection. If the conversion experience includes consciousness of the presence

[1] *The Psychology of Religion*, by G. A. Coe. Chicago: University of Chicago Press, 1916, p. 153.

of the Christian God, it is because Christian rather than, say, Brahmin ideas of God have already been acquired. Only so does Christian 'assurance' or 'the witness of the Spirit' occur in any articulate sense."

Secondly, on the other hand, fresh sensory elements often play a part in conversion. "The tone of a preacher's voice; the rhythm, melody, and volume of revival songs; repetition of a given impression; the sight of others performing a religious act; organic sensations, such as thrills, tingles, shudders; very possibly now and then sexual sensations not recognised as such; and the entire sensory mass that constitutes physical tone, particularly fatigue and similar states in which excitability as distinguished from discriminative sensibility exist — all these have to be reckoned with."

Thirdly, certain instinctive impulses are present. "Instinct plays a part in conversions. Many revivals are instances of gregariousness, that is, of a coming together because the mere presence of others gives satisfaction. Then, disapproval from others produces distress, and approval produces satisfaction, altogether apart from any judgment that one might form on other grounds as to one's own conduct or character. Thus the group standard passes over into individual conviction and determination partly by an instinctive route. Further, instinctive submission to the assertive personality of an evangelist, or to the Church as greater than the individual, or to the overpowering greatness and goodness of God."

Fourthly, Coe notes "a law under which these elements are characteristically combined." Conversion is a process of self-realisation for the subject himself. "The sense of emancipation is a sense of being where free selves are at home; the convert's new world has the standpoint of the convert himself; it is suffused with the self-enlarging, self-emancipating principle . . . Granted that his training has prepared him for the crisis, and that conversion puts him under the control of existing social standards and ideas of God, the fact remains that conversion makes these things real to the convert. Heretofore he had 'knowledge about' them; now he has 'acquaintance with' them. The world or God has meaning *for him* and makes response *now*. Here is no mere repetition of the past, for the individual is a new and unique one, and this experience *as his* is as fresh as the creation morn itself." [1]

These extracts from Dr. Coe are quoted at length because they sum up succinctly and accurately the findings from our own research. The stimulus–organism–response formula, familiar to psychology, holds good in conversion as in any other personal experience. The stimulus may be a Church service, a meeting, a sermon, a challenge from a friend, the repetition of an earlier situation with religious associations, and so forth; but every conversion involves a personal and individual reaction or response, and the individual is likely to respond in ways characteristic of himself as a person. For example, the child nurtured in a Christian home, and who has not known the depths of sin, will make a different response from the man who has had little or no religious training and whose greatest temptations are drink and moral vice. Some will look to Christ as the Bearer of their sins; some will follow Him as their Leader and Guide through life; some will fall at His feet as Lord and Master; some will turn to Him as Friend; some will trust Him as Deliverer; some will just accept Him without realising the precise implications of their response.

The Process of Re-birth

A phenomenon I have noticed in relation to adult conversions may be termed *a return to childhood experiences*. In some cases there is a definite return to childhood levels of response. The sound of a hymn being sung in the distance,

[1] G. A. Coe, *Psychology of Religion*, pp. 152–74.

or a phrase heard in a sermon, or some otherwise trivial occurrence, will sometimes set in motion a chain of associations, which bring to the subject's mind experiences of his childhood days and early teaching that had long been "forgotten". Adult converts have been known to begin their new life by repeating the prayers which they learnt as children. In such cases the conversion would seem to be, from the psychological point of view, a re-birth of ideas and ideals unconsciously, if not consciously, held in earlier days. I offer two examples:

A man of over sixty years of age gave his witness in my presence. He told a moving story. His testimony was as follows: As a child he was sent to Sunday School. He said that his mother was a godly woman, though his father made no religious profession. The subject himself departed in his later youth from his mother's ways, lived selfishly and recklessly, and eventually became involved in crime for which he was imprisoned. He told how, during his first night in prison, he began to think over his past life. The years rolled back, and in imagination he was once again in his old homestead. He thought of his mother (now long since dead), and recalled her life of simple piety. He thought and thought, until suddenly he found himself kneeling on the floor and crying: "Gentle Jesus, meek and mild, look upon a little child; pity my simplicity, suffer me to come to Thee. Amen." And that prayer, which his mother had taught him, spoken almost spontaneously but with deep emotion, was the beginning of a new life for him.

A man in middle life who found himself in trouble, involved in a situation brought about by his own wrong-doing, testifies that he was brought to the point of conversion when he realised that a conflict was raging within between the "self" of his childhood, with its noble ideals and aims, and the miserable person he now was, seared and spoiled by the circumstances of a profligate life. Seeking forgiveness for the past, he surrendered to his "better self", took up the nobler life from where he left it in childhood, and by that process found victory and release. In a true sense he was "born again", and "came to himself". It would be interesting to gather more data on this aspect of adult conversion. I believe it to be an important factor in a number of cases.

The Element of Self-Judgment and Rejection

In some cases of conversion there is an element of self-judgment and rejection of the past. Sometimes, as in the case of so-called "hardened sinners", the rejection is natural and necessary. But sometimes one finds an irrational and unnecessary rejection and self-condemnation. I heard a young man of eighteen years of age giving his testimony. He began by telling us that he had been nurtured in a religious home, that his parents were exemplary Christians, and that he had been brought up to go to church, to say his prayers, and to read his Bible every day. At the age of sixteen he began Sunday School teaching. "But, friends," he said, "I was not converted. I did not know Jesus Christ as my own personal Saviour. My friends thought that I was a Christian, but I was not. I was a wicked, hell-deserving sinner. My heart was black. Black! God alone knows how black my heart was." And so on. We might dismiss it as the extravagant language of an enthusiastic youth, but this was a testimony given in a public service during a special mission effort. It was said with great feeling and earnestness. The young man was sincere, and obviously believed what he said.

The element of self-judgment and rejection is not always so naïve or so vocal, but it is often there under the surface. Sometimes it remains as a more or less permanent characteristic of the new life; and sometimes its intensity is lessened by the time process, and in later life the subject shows fewer signs of rejection and even begins to incorporate into the new life some of the characteristics of the past, and thus achieves a deeper level of personal integration.

Dr. Routley describes conversion as "a radical renewal" and a complete reorientation. As a new-born child of God, the convert looks back upon his past life and realises with shame its shortcomings. A vital point made by Dr. Routley is that, theologically speaking, conversion follows the pattern of Christ's Death and Resurrection. The convert "dies" to the old life and "rises" to the new. The gift enshrined in the miracle of conversion is the gift of New Life in Christ. It follows the pattern of — Death: Resurrection: The Power of the New Life in the Holy Spirit. Routley says: "Even Pentecost is there in the irresistible impulse in the converted man to go forth and tell the good news to all his neighbours." I think that this is a most important insight. It throws considerable light on this phenomenon of self-judgment and rejection which we have here been considering.

Conformity to the In-group

Closely associated with the element of rejection — the obverse side of the element of rejection, so to speak — is a tendency to conform to the new in-group to whom allegiance is given. Conversion soon gives to the subject a sense of "belonging" to the family of converted people. I have known a few "outsiders" to be converted. In the early days of their association with the Christian group, their approach to religious matters was both original and refreshing. Their language was so unsophisticated, and their ideas so challenging. But in every case, I have noticed that before long they have begun to adopt the vocabulary and ideas of the in-group, and so have come to conform to its thought-forms and to the pattern of its life. Where the conversion involves anything like a violent break with the past, this tendency to conform to the ideas and ways of the new in-group appears to be associated with a need for assurance. The change wrought by the conversion demands a new adjustment to life, and this tendency to conform seems almost like an unconscious attempt to assure the self that *now* it is right, or safe, or complete, or satisfied. In theological language it is ceasing to be "conformed to this world", and being "transformed by the renewing of the mind" so as to "prove what is that good, and acceptable, and perfect, will of God." [1]

Now this tendency to conform may be a good or a bad thing, according to the use that is made of it by the subject and by the group. It is a desirable development if it leads the subject to an autonomous acceptance of Christian standards in the place of lower standards of behaviour; but it is an undesirable thing if it means for him simply the learning of new "shiboleths" and leads to the loss of individuality or autonomy. And Bishop Stephen Neill [2] has shown the danger inherent in all group movements, of substituting adherence to the group for vital, personal experience.

These, then, are the main psychological mechanisms of conversion: The conditioning process, a response characteristic of the individual, the process of re-birth, the element of self-judgment and rejection, and a tendency to conform to the life pattern of the in-group. These processes are to some degree present in all cases of conversion, though individuals differ in the degree of their manifestation. The final stage of religious conversion is characterised by a sense of peace and of reconciliation with reality. A sense of calm pervades the mind as the subject becomes assured of forgiveness for the past, of life in the present, and of power for the future. Although in one sense conversion is only the first step in the religious life, only the first stage of the spiritual pilgrimage, there is always an element of assurance about it, a feeling of having "arrived".

[1] Romans 12 : 2.
[2] "Conversion", by Bishop Stephen C. Neill, in *Scottish Journal of Theology*, Vol. 3, No. 4, December, 1950, p. 361.

Chapter Four

PROBLEMS IN RELATION TO
RELIGIOUS CONVERSION

STEREOTYPING THE CONVERSION PROCESS

GUILT INDUCTION

INDUCEMENT OF FEAR

THE LAPSED CONVERT

UNDUE SOCIAL PRESSURE

PREMATURE DECISION

LACK OF PASTORAL CARE

ETHICAL STANDARDS IN EVANGELISM

PROBLEMS IN RELATION TO
RELIGIOUS CONVERSION

PRESSING for conversions, especially in the context of large-scale missions and other special evangelistic efforts, has its problems and dangers as well as its successes; and it is necessary that these should be examined. There are ethical considerations in relation to evangelism that are not always borne in mind by the enthusiastic evangelist; and there are also theological questions in regard to the evangelistic message which ought to be considered. My anecdotes here may be considered illustrations of an extreme kind, but they illumine common dangers and pitfalls that beset any would-be evangelist. They are not atypical: these stories could be duplicated by many an experienced pastor or evangelist.

Stereotyping the Conversion Process

Dr. Routley has some important things to say on this point. He says that there has grown up a "mythology of conversion". It is frequently thought that all conversions follow a fairly general pattern. There are archetypes of conversion. These are the well-known and authentic stories which everybody knows either by acquaintance with the sources or by hearsay. The three pre-eminent archetypes are St. Paul, St. Augustine, and John Wesley. They all had "similar" conversions. Dr. Routley, however, demonstrates that, for all their similarities, they are really quite different. He says: "All they have in common is that they are a turning to the Christian Way. But in all other matters they differ *toto caelo*. Paul turns from persecuting the Way. Augustine turns

from insulting it. Wesley turns from following it blindfold.
Paul is a man of learning, Augustine a cultivated man of
licence, Wesley a man of piety. Paul, converted, becomes an
apostle; Augustine, converted, becomes a bishop and man of
letters (in some respects, not the best of bishops); Wesley,
converted, becomes a missionary to his home country. You
cannot even use the three stories to clericalize conversion;
only Augustine of the three becomes anything essentially
like a professional minister of the Gospel." [1]

The dangers of stereotyping the process of conversion
came home to me vividly a few years ago when I had the
opportunity to observe a professional evangelist in his approach to individual "inquirers" at the close of his evangelistic services. For his own guidance he had drawn up a series
of Bible texts which he felt adequately summed up "the way
of salvation". These included:

"All have sinned, and come short of the glory of God"
(Romans 3: 23);

"The wages of sin is death" (Romans 6: 23);

"The soul that sinneth, it shall die" (Ezekiel 18: 4);

"But God commendeth his love toward us, in that, while
we were yet sinners, Christ died for us" (Romans 5: 8);

"Him that cometh to me I will in no wise cast out" (St.
John 6: 37);

"He that believeth on the Son hath everlasting life: and he
that believeth not the Son shall not see life; but the wrath of
God abideth on him" (St. John 3: 36);

"Behold, I stand at the door, and knock: if any man hear
my voice, and open the door, I will come in" (Revelation
3: 20).

These were the texts the evangelist would use time and
time again as one and another came into the vestry to seek
his help. His sermon might have been from the Old Testa-
ment, or from the Gospels, or from some doctrinal passage

[1] *The Gift of Conversion*, p. 26.

from St. Paul; and the "inquirer" might be a man or woman, young or old, educated or uneducated; but the evangelist's method was always the same. Here was a soul seeking salvation. Here was the "plan of salvation". All he felt that he needed to do was to apply the "plan" to the person. There was hardly ever any conversation about the inquirer's background, or the steps which had led him (or her) to make this approach to the evangelist. The inquirer was simply taken step by step through the evangelist's carefully prepared "plan of salvation", and at the end was asked: "Will *you* believe? Will you let Christ come in to-night?" He would then lead the inquirer in a prayer which had become almost completely stereotyped by constant use, at the end of which the "convert" would be asked to sign a Decision Card. His name and address would be recorded for follow-up purposes, and he would be bowed out whilst the next "inquirer" was shown in, the evangelist meanwhile rejoicing over "another soul brought to Jesus."

Now, in fairness to that particular evangelist, let me add that, to my knowledge, some, at least, of his converts have "stood". But, on the other hand, I must record that they did not all stand, and that, on the whole, he was working amongst folk who had been reared in a definitely evangelical atmosphere. On the whole, he was addressing his message to minds that had been conditioned to receive it, and after their "decision" they had to go on to work out their own salvation and to grow in grace.

There is no harm in an evangelist preparing himself beforehand, or in his having certain Bible passages memorised in anticipation of his being able to help someone by their use. Any propagandist, whatever his theme might be, would do the same. But there are dangers in it, and if pressed too far it can have an adverse effect, not only upon the individual inquirer, but upon the whole cause which the evangelist seeks to serve.

E

Guilt Induction

Closely associated with the temptation to stereotype the conversion process, there is another temptation to which certain evangelists appear to be exposed. That is, the temptation to attempt to create in their hearers a sensitivity to a particular kind of need. Usually, what the evangelist is trying to create is a "conviction of sin". The aim appears to be to create a sense of need in respect of guilt-consciousness, and then to offer the evangel as the answer to that need. Dr. William Sargant's work is a commentary on this kind of evangelism.

This introduces a difficult and ticklish question. Can there be any true conversion without a prior conviction of sin? This matter has come under discussion several times recently in evangelical circles. It is sometimes said by evangelistically minded people that the greatest need of our generation is a conviction of sin. A renewed interest in the revivals of the past has produced in some a longing for a repetition in our own day of the phenomena of those revivals. I have heard it said that in the great revivals of the eighteenth and nineteenth centuries "even children came under deep conviction of sin." That is true, but we need to see the phenomenon in its true perspective. We have already seen that these revivals were related to contemporary religious thought, and those who are familiar with the literature of the period know how strong was the emphasis upon the sinfulness of sin. These were children whose minds had been conditioned to feel guilt-conscious.

As reported in Chapter Two, conviction of sin is still widely felt amongst those who are nurtured in a religious atmosphere. The question I am raising here is: Is this conviction of sin essential to real conversion? It is not sufficient answer to say that in the past a wide-spread conviction has always been a characteristic of revival, or to argue that to-day the majority of converts do, at some point in their experience, feel a sense of sin, and that the majority turn to Christ as their personal Saviour and Redeemer. Of course they do, for hitherto the evangelistic message has been confined to the themes of sin (including also the idea of judgment), atonement, and the Saviourhood of Christ. The cynic may suggest that the converts have experienced what they have been conditioned to expect. On the other hand, the evangelist may argue that he must preach sin, atonement, and Christ's Saviourhood, because these *are* the Gospel. These constitute the evangel. They are at the heart of the good news which he is commissioned to proclaim.

But that is precisely the question. Is the preaching of sin, atonement, and the Saviourhood of Christ a sufficient basis for evangelism to-day? My own experience and research have convinced me that individuals make their own response in their own way, and that not all the saints pass through the same psychological mould. I would suggest that here is a problem which ought to be discussed widely and fully, with all the theological competence, psychological insight, and practical experience that is available. And in this connection, I would recommend a thoughtful reading of Alan Walker's book, *The Whole Gospel for the Whole World*, mentioned previously, in which he argues most powerfully and reasonably that nineteenth century evangelism is not adequate for twentieth century needs.

Sometimes, as we have seen, a subject will convert when he gets a vision of his better self, and this aspect of the case must be borne in mind when discussing the element of conviction. "I am convinced we often fail to win men," wrote the saintly George Matheson,[1] "just because we suggest to them their badness rather than their goodness. It is a fatal thing for a man when he comes to feel that nobody believes

[1] *Messages of Hope*, by George Matheson. London: James Clarke & Co. Ltd., pp. 110–11.

in him . . . A bad man is never so near to repentance as when he is surprised into a good action. It is from hope, not from despair, that the sting of conscience comes. I am never ashamed of myself till I see what I *might* have been. When does the man of Tarsus fall to the earth? When he gets a vision of his better self — when the voice of Christ says to him, 'I am surprised that a man like you should not have been on my side; Saul, Saul, why persecutest thou me!' "

I once ministered for some weeks to a dying man, though he was said not to know that he was dying. He was very far from being a religious man, though he obviously wanted to talk about religion. One day he said to me: "Mister, I'm not the good man you think I am, *but I want to be*." Within minutes we were talking about his childhood, his home-life, the religious ideals he had imbibed from his parents in those far-off days. He did the talking, and as he spoke the crust of years fell away, and the little child — simple, trustful, wondering — emerged. I was conscious of witnessing a re-birth; and in that child-like faith he eventually died.

Inducement of Fear

In Chapter Two we referred to the part which fear plays as a factor in conversion. There is a sense of fear — a desire for security, for example — which seems to be a natural stage in the spiritual development of a large number of people. But sometimes evangelists are tempted to make too much of it. In several instances subjects have told me that at the time of their conversion the evangelist sought to instil fear into their hearts, but that they were aware of this and resisted it.

This raises another ticklish question, but someone must raise it. Our generation is living under a cloud of fear; it is not surprising, therefore, to find that fear is one of the elements in a large number of conversions. But has the evangelist any right to prey upon it? Both in the past and in the present day, evangelists have used the threat of national disaster as a platform for Gospel-preaching. But is this legitimate? Is the use of fear-producing techniques ever justified in evangelism? I doubt it. The evangelist's message is one of love, grace, tenderness, compassion. There is no need to introduce the element of fear unnaturally; and to do so is unworthy and ethically unjustifiable.

The Lapsed Convert

Finally, there is the problem of lapses. Twenty years ago, Dr. Eric S. Waterhouse computed that not more than 20 per cent of those who professed conversion proved satisfactory.[1] Whether more recent efforts will prove more lasting in their effects, it is too early to judge. In a recent article in the *British Weekly*, the Reverend Cecil Northcott [2] quoted figures from a survey made by the *Evening Standard* in December, 1954, eight months after Dr. Billy Graham's Harringay Campaign had finished. There were about 36,000 converts from this campaign; 24,000 of them were "old faithfuls"; and of the other 12,000, fewer than 4,000 were still in the churches.

Attached to the same article were figures showing the numerical impact of the Graham campaign on twenty London churches, and the same overall pattern is observable. Of 336 inquirers, 226 were described as "old church-goers", and 110 as "outsiders". Of these 110 outsiders, only 35 were still to be found in the churches.

Of course, the total effect of any campaign cannot be assessed in terms of numerical impact alone, and in quoting these figures one does not wish to imply any criticism either

[1] *Psychology and Pastoral Work*, by Eric S. Waterhouse. London: Hodder & Stoughton Ltd., 1939, p. 143.
[2] "Four Years after Billy Graham", by Cecil Northcott, in *the British Weekly*, 29th May, 1958.

of Billy Graham himself or of the clergy and members of the churches who received his converts. In fairness to all concerned, it must be recorded that Dr. Graham and all who were associated with him were most careful to ensure the following-up of inquirers, and that many clergy and ministers faithfully did their part. Not much more could have been done in the way of organisation. And I wish to make it clear, also, that what I have to say under this heading has no reference to these particular churches and converts, or, indeed, to any one particular campaign. My purpose in quoting these figures is, rather, to illustrate the fact that, even after all possible care has been taken to ensure the stability of the converts, and when all the machinery of modern organisation is geared to that end, the number of lapses is still high.

The problem of lapses must be faced. In connection with a recent campaign I was told that those who were preparing for it were praying that 50 per cent of the converts might stand. In anticipation of the campaign they had judged that a fifty-fifty result would be satisfactory. Frankly, I was appalled. Experience has taught me that untold harm could be done to the 50 per cent who were expected to lapse. No man has the right to traffic thus in souls. The professional evangelist, particularly, is in danger of harming souls by the very methods that he is expected to employ for success in his work — as many an experienced pastor or parish priest can testify. But this danger is not to be regarded as associated only with the work of the professional evangelist; it is present whenever one person seeks to persuade another to make the great decision.

If we inquire: What are the reasons for so many lapses? we are asking a question which cannot be answered simply. But personal contact with some who have lapsed, together with a careful study of the spiritual histories of some who had partially lapsed, or who had lapsed for a time, and were restored by the experience which we have earlier termed "secondary conversion" or "re-conversion", suggests certain reasons which ought to be considered in a work of this nature. A "lapse" is, in essence, failure on the part of the individual convert to achieve full integration with, and conformity to, the new pattern of life, so that he returns to his former way of living. This may be due to various factors within the convert himself. Jesus knew this, and illustrated it in his parable of the Sower.[1] Jesus taught there that superficiality, shallowness, and compromise with the old life are causes of spiritual unfruitfulness.

Now all this is true, of course, and sometimes a "convert" who has lapsed will be honest enough to admit that he fell away because he could not face the demands which the new way of life made upon him. But the first cause of the lapse does not by any means always rest with the convert himself. Frequently it lies with the evangelist or with the circumstances of the conversion experience. Dr. D. Martyn Lloyd-Jones has recently expressed concern over this point.[2] My own studies have led me to conclude that there are, possibly, three main reasons, apart from those mentioned above, which account for many lapses. They are: (1) Undue social pressure; (2) premature decision; and (3) lack of pastoral care. These problems are so important that they deserve to be considered fully in sections of their own.

Undue Social Pressure

In mass or group evangelism there is always the danger of undue emotionalism due to social pressure. Of course, there is a certain emotional content in every religious experience, and no one can be converted without *feeling* it. But there is a real danger of decisions based too much upon the emotions, wherever the Gospel preaching is reinforced

[1] St. Matthew 13: 1–9; 16–23.
[2] *Conversions, Psychological and Spiritual*, by D. Martyn Lloyd-Jones. London: Inter-Varsity Fellowship Press, 1959.

either by the largeness of the crowd or by the enthusiasm of the group. Every professional evangelist knows the power of social pressure (though every evangelist would not call it by that name), and that is one reason why he asks for the prayers and moral support of so many persons.

But social pressure definitely has its dangers. It is a commonplace to remark that the individual tends to become lost in a crowd. Imitation, sympathy, and suggestibility are heightened in a crowd or group, and the individual becomes susceptible to the moods of the group. If the group stimulus is strong, the individual may experience a profound alteration in his mental activity. His normal reactions tend to be modified; he becomes credulous and open to influence; his emotions are intensified, intellectual ability is reduced, and the will is easily swayed in the direction of an approximation to the other individuals in the group. Anyone who wishes to make an impression on a crowd can do so by the judicious use of choice phrases and by exaggeration. Much depends upon the leader.

Now, all this is common psychological knowledge, but it has a bearing upon the problem under discussion. Sometimes a decision made in a crowd or group, or in other unusual circumstances, is too highly emotional and is subsequently regretted. The emotional "atmosphere" of the evangelistic meeting and the persuasiveness of the preacher or personal worker lead to a "decision" which is psychologically inadequate. The decision is made without due thought and without the full assent of the will. Something less than the whole personality is, therefore, involved in the act, and in time the decision is regretted and reversed.

There is no doubt that this is one reason for some lapses.

Premature Decision

In some cases the "convert" has been pressed to make a decision prematurely. Such a decision cannot be regarded as satisfactory from the point of view either of the "convert" or of the Church, and in the long run it does not enhance the reputation of the evangelist. In time it is almost certain to have unfortunate results.

For example, a youth attended regularly a weekly Young People's Service. He was interested and impressed, but not convinced. One night, after the service, he was pressed (against his will) by an over-zealous worker to remain behind and to make a profession in the presence of several others. He left the Hall that night never to return. Examples like this could be multiplied.

Often a premature decision means a superficial conversion. This is particularly so in the case of child-conversions. So often, in an evangelical atmosphere, a child makes a response. Adults read into his response more than the child understands, and henceforth treat the child like a young adult, a mature believer. This creates a state of tension in the child's mind, for he finds himself expected to adopt attitudes and to accept responsibilities which are beyond him, and which he did not anticipate when he made his open response to the Gospel. In later life he begins to doubt whether he is converted at all. Unless he is closely linked to the Christian fellowship, he is likely to lapse. On the other hand, his very integration into the life of the fellowship, and all that is expected of him by the fellowship, sometimes even increases his state of inner tension. I give but one example:

A boy of ten years of age (let us call him James), attended an evangelistic service for adults. At the close of the service he was persuaded to "give his heart to Jesus". He made the profession that was expected of him, but that profession was the beginning of years of conflict within. At the end of the interview, the evangelist extracted from him a promise with regard to his future habits and manner of life — a promise which involved far more than James realised at the time. Being a conscientious boy, James kept his promise; but there came a time in later adolescence when he regretted that promise, and reproved himself for having made it. He wanted to break it, yet felt afraid and ashamed to do so. In his early "twenties" he found himself in a state of mental and spiritual turmoil. He would have given up religion, but he felt himself too involved in it to extricate himself from it. His tension was resolved by psychological treatment. All his troubles stemmed from the fact that *at the time of his conversion, he had been made to profess too much and too soon.* And one wonders how many other child-converts are put into such an unfair and false position by well-meaning adults who do not understand the child mind. It is all too easy to persuade children — and adults, for that matter — to make a decision before they are psychologically and spiritually prepared.

One more example, of another type: A woman who had not had the advantage of a Christian upbringing, at a time of personal anxiety and sorrow turned to a friend, who happened to be a Christian, for help. The Christian friend took her to church where for the first time in her life she heard the story of God's love. She became a seeker and a learner, but she had much to learn and could not reconcile what she heard with her own painful experience of suffering. About this time she attended an evangelistic mission. One night the evangelist asked her, "Are you saved?" She replied that she was not, but that she was a seeker. Whereupon, without further questioning, and with little display of sympathy, he urged her to make her decision immediately, emphasizing the peril of delay. She refused, and almost gave up her seeking as a result of the encounter. Years after the incident she revealed that it had shocked her. She said: "I was so amazed at his lack of understanding that I nearly gave up seeking Christ. However, the sense of my need prevailed and at last I came to Christ." Had she "come" when the evangelist urged her, her decision would have been premature, and, more likely than not, unsatisfactory.

Lack of Pastoral Care

Some lapses are due to the simple fact that the converts are not "followed up". This is a matter which is receiving thought and attention, but it is worth mentioning here. It is a problem frequently associated with large-scale missions, but it is not confined to them. All too often, a false impression is given by those who press the claims of the Gospel upon others. I once knew a lady to lapse simply because at the time of her conversion, when she was passing through a period of personal stress and suffering, the evangelist had declared that if only she would come to Christ, all her problems would be solved, and life would be completely happy and victorious. Unfortunately, the evangelist had not reckoned with a personal situation which the poor woman was quite unable to change, and which would have tried the greatest saint. The evangelist's promises were too glib; they did not mature, and the poor misguided "convert" lapsed. What she needed was the care and assistance of a pastor who could help her to adjust her faith to her circumstances. The evangelist, in this instance, failed to help the woman at the real point of her need.

In like manner, lapses occur, sometimes, for the simple reason that the circumstances surrounding the conversion experience are too unlike the normal circumstances of the subject's everyday life, and there is no one to help him to make the necessary adjustment. For example, a boy converted in camp may have to return to a situation which is very different from the happy, care-free, holiday atmosphere, where all appear to be Christians — and exuberant Christians, at that! — and where it is comparatively easy to conform to the pattern of the religious life. Such a boy needs far more help than is often accorded him.

Or, again, a person converted in an "evangelical" atmosphere may find difficulty in relating this experience to the main general pattern of his religious life, if that pattern happens to be one where conversion is not particularly emphasized. I knew a youth who was converted in an evangelical fellowship. He went back to his own vicar to tell him the good news. But to the vicar it was bad news. He pooh-poohed the idea, and poured scorn on the trouble-making enthusiasts who had been seeking to influence a member of his flock. He told the youth that he did not believe in conversion. No wonder the young man found himself in a state of tension. What was he to do? One clergyman believed in conversion, and another did not. The easiest thing for him to do was to lapse.

Ethical Standards in Evangelism

Before closing this section, I desire to make an appeal for the raising of the general ethical standards of popular evangelism. But first let me state that I do fully acknowledge the sincerity, the earnestness, and the competence of many who are engaged in the preaching and teaching of the Gospel. To such I apologise if my appeal appears to involve them; though I fancy that they would be amongst the first to support the appeal I am about to make.

Some of the methods currently in use in the work of evangelism are not beyond reproof. I could write a whole chapter on abuses, but would hesitate to make public some of the details I have accumulated. I appeal to all who engage in evangelism — whether as professional evangelists, Sunday School teachers, Bible Class leaders, camp "officers", or simply as individual Christians making their witness to others — to use all restraint, and to spurn the use of mass-suggestion techniques and other "tricks of the trade" to obtain conversions. After all, the work they are attempting is worthy of the highest and best methods; and the highest motives demand the highest ethical standards in their achievement.

One great danger to which all evangelical workers are exposed, is the temptation to look for converts and therefore of pressing for decisions. Indeed, converts are the justification of the existence of the evangelist. But it is a grave error. The evangelist (be he professional evangelist, camp leader, or other kind of evangelist) comes and goes; it is the parish clergyman or the resident minister who has the more difficult task; and, unfortunately, some clergy and ministers know from bitter experience the trail of mishandled religious experiences which an unwise or an unscrupulous evangelist can leave behind.

These, then, are some of the main problems, as I see them: The tendency to stereotype the conversion process; the temptation to induce unduly a sense of guilt and/or fear; undue social pressure resulting in over-emotional conversions; the dangers of premature decisions; and the problems associated with the lack of pastoral care. And in addition we have to admit that there is, in some quarters, room for improvement in the ethical standards adopted. These are pressing problems, and problems which call for the most careful consideration possible. Until they are faced more widely, much of our evangelism will remain unsatisfactory.

Chapter Five

TOWARDS A THEOLOGY OF CONVERSION

CONVERSION AS THE EPITOME OR FOCUS
OF THE RELIGIOUS LIFE

THE HUMAN ELEMENT IN CONVERSION

CONVERSION IN RELATION TO BAPTISM
AND REGENERATION

TOWARDS A THEOLOGY OF
CONVERSION

THUS far, our attention has been focused upon the psychological and pastoral aspects of conversion. Our study would not be complete, however, without reference to the theological aspect. It is my conviction that the time has come for us to re-think our theology of conversion in the light of all available knowledge. This is not a new plea. Both Bishop Stephen Neill [1] and Dr. D. Martyn Lloyd-Jones,[2] writing from different points of view, have called attention to the need for a theological approach to the study of conversion. Dr. B. Citron [3] has done us a great service by setting forth clearly the view-points of various theological systems on the subject. The Archbishop of Cape Town [4] and the Reverend Douglas Webster [5] have both contributed to one aspect of the problem — namely, the relation of Baptism to Conversion — and Canon Theodore O. Wedel [6] has contributed to the discussion at the ecumenical level.

It would be beyond the purpose of this little book to attempt to supply a theology of conversion. This chapter,

[1] "Conversion", *Scottish Journal of Theology*, p. 352.
[2] *Conversions, Psychological and Spiritual*, pp. 26 ff.
[3] *New Birth: A Study of the Evangelical Doctrine of Conversion in the Protestant Fathers*, by B. Citron. Edinburgh: The University Press, pp. 124–44.
[4] *This is Conversion*, pp. 41 ff.
[5] *What is Conversion?* pp. 163 ff.
[6] "Evangelism an Essay in Criticism", *The Ecumenical Review*, Vol. III, No. 4, July, 1951; and "Evangelism's Threefold Witness: Kerygma, Koinonia, Diakonia", *The Ecumenical Review*, Vol. IX, No. 3, 1957. Both articles by Canon Theodore O. Wedel.

as its title implies, is intended, rather, to indicate those factors which my own studies have led me to believe are important in arriving at such a theology.

Conversion as the Epitome or Focus of the Religious Life

When E. D. Starbuck began his study into what he called "the line of growth in religion in individuals", he quickly saw that conversion epitomises the experience of religious development. As he said, conversion "seems to show in a condensed form some of the essential features of religious development." He recognised that in countless cases, conversion is a perfectly normal psychologic crisis, marking the transition from the child's world to the wider world of youth, or from that of youth to that of maturity, and that it is "a crisis which the evangelical machinery only methodically emphasizes, abridges, and regulates."

This would seem to be important as a starting-point for any theology of conversion. Dr. Routley [1] helps us here, too. Conversion is always on the pattern of the Incarnation, Cross and Resurrection, and Pentecost. The convert "dies" to the old life and "rises" to the new. "The gift enshrined in the miracle" of conversion "is the gift of New Life" in Christ, he says, and it follows the pattern of Death — Resurrection — the Power of the New Life in the Holy Spirit.

The Human Element in Conversion

One difficulty in framing a theology of conversion is that as soon as we begin to apply theological concepts to it, we find ourselves involved in the use of mystical language, as, for example, when we speak of the convert "dying and rising with Christ". Perhaps the use of such language is inevitable, but from the view-point of scientific analysis it can be misleading.

[1] *The Gift of Conversion*, p. 53.

We must never forget that, in essence, conversion is *a human act*. It is a man's response to particular religious stimuli. A man *converts*, rather than *is converted*. It is only when we recognise this that we can begin to formulate accurate propositions; and it is only in so far as it describes factual experience that mystical language can have any significant meaning.

When E. D. Starbuck began his pioneer work into the psychological study of conversion, he had to answer the charge of impiety. He wrote: "Those . . . who hold conceptions which separate sharply the spiritual realm from the mundane, who acknowledge law and the consequent validity of science in the one, but set the other under the control of voluntary and arbitrary decrees, will look on a scientific study of religion with distrust and suspicion. In fact, during the years that these studies in the psychology of religion have been in progress the warning has often been given in good faith that we are entering upon a hopeless quest. The ways of God, it is said, are beyond human comprehension. 'The wind bloweth where it listeth and thou hearest the sound thereof, but canst not tell whence it cometh or whither it goeth, so is everyone that is born of the Spirit', is the oft-repeated quotation . . . The growth of science has been a growth of the recognition of law. A little while ago comets and meteors were heralds of good or ill to man; historical events were the sequence of juxtaposition of planets or flight of birds; sickness, misfortune, and death were visitations of divine displeasure — and science under such conditions was impossible. Now, in the physical world, caprice and chance have been eliminated. All things follow an irresistible sequence of cause and effect . . . The meteorologist is even studying the wind, and with some degree of success is finding whence it comes and whither it goes . . . The fundamental assumption [of the psychology of religion] is that religion is a real fact of human experience, and develops according to law. Although these laws are peculiar to their own sphere, and need not harmonise readily with those of physics, chemistry, and the like, nevertheless, the facts have an order which, given wisdom enough, may be ascertained. The service of psychology to practical religion is to make possible a harvest of wiser means in moral and religious culture, and also to lift religion sufficiently out of the domain of feeling to make it appeal to the understanding, so that it may become possible, progressively, to appreciate its truth and apperceive its essential elements." [1]

The humanness of the act of converting is illustrated (1) by the fact that conversions are known in religions other than Christianity, as Dr. A. C. Underwood has shown; [2] (2) by the experience known sometimes as counter-conversion, which J. B. Pratt describes as "the sudden and emotional turning away from Christianity and religion", which "may follow much the same psychological course as the conventional conversion experience"; [3] and (3) by the fact that, as an individual's response, conversion is conditioned by a number of factors, as, for example, upbringing, type of religious instruction received, and antecedent experiences. At the moment of writing, I am engaged on further research on this last point, so will say no more about it at this stage; but it does emphasize the fact that, in examining conversion we are analysing an essentially human phenomenon.

All this means that, in arriving at a theology of conversion, we must consider more than many of us have tended to do in the past, the characteristically *human* elements in the conversion experience. Indeed, perhaps we must make more allowance than is customary for the human element in all religious experience.

[1] *The Psychology of Religion*, pp. 1–17.
[2] *Conversion: Christian and Non-Christian*.
[3] *The Religious Consciousness*, by J. B. Pratt. New York: The Macmillan Company, 1941, pp. 126–7.

Conversion in relation to Baptism and Regeneration

Such an approach might begin to solve some of our more academic problems, for example, that of the relationship between conversion and Baptism. I should welcome correspondence on this point, for I am gathering data in regard to it. I should be grateful to learn the views of others; and perhaps it might be possible to collate the relevant data and present them in some ordered form at a later date. This is more than an academic question. It is an important practical question for the day-to-day pastoral ministry.

Here I offer only a tentative suggestion. Perhaps it is some solution to say that conversion — unconscious or conscious; sudden, gradual, or in stages—is an individual's acknowledgment of the position in which his baptism has placed him. This still leaves open the question: What happens at Baptism? Perhaps this question needs to be answered first; but for the moment, i.e. in the present context, it does not seem to matter how we answer that question. If we say that at Baptism the child is dedicated to God, then conversion could be interpreted as the adolescent's (or the adult's) acknowledgment of this relationship to God. If we say that the infant was regenerated by a supernatural gift, then conversion could be the realisation, on the part of the subject, of the possession of that gift. But this only takes into consideration Infant Baptism. What relationship are we to find between Adult Baptism and conversion? There is, obviously a wide field for discussion here.

A question I have often been asked in regard to what is here termed "conversion by stages" is: At what stage, would you say, is the individual converted? Immediately, and without hesitation, I have always replied at the very first stage. I believe that when an individual turns, and makes a committal, *that* is his conversion. He is in the Way. All subsequent stages are but signs that he has been progressing along the Way. To hold any other view would, I believe, be psychologically unsound and pastorally disastrous.

These, then, are some of the facts and factors which appear to be important in the formulation of any theological theory concerning conversion. This is an urgent matter, and it is to be hoped that more constructive thought will be given to it in the near future.

Chapter Six

CONVERSION IN PERSPECTIVE

CONVERSION AND PERSONAL RELIGION

CONVERSION AND THE WORK OF THE CHURCH

POSTSCRIPT

CONVERSION IN PERSPECTIVE

It is important to get this matter of conversion in perspective. There are still clergy who "do not believe in conversion", or who regard it as a concomitant of a particular form of obscurantist fundamentalism. It is, of course, nothing of the sort. It is a well-authenticated fact of human experience confined to no particular religious body or sect. On the other hand, the current revival of interest in the Church's evangelistic task, has produced a wide-spread feeling amongst clergy and lay people of another type, that conversion is the one essential religious experience. What we need is a balanced view of the matter, and this we shall arrive at only by patient and thoughtful consideration of all that it involves both for the individual and for the Church. Here we shall consider conversion, first in the perspective of personal religious experience, and then in its corporate setting in relation to the work of the Church.

Conversion and Personal Religion

In the first place, we must consider the fact of conversion in the context of personal religious experience. It is evident that religious development follows the pattern of all normal human progress. There appear to be three phases of development, not really separable, but vitally related, in the normal growth of the individual from childhood to maturity; and these hold good whether we consider ordinary human development or the development of the religious life:

(1) First, in early childhood, there is a period of simple

credulity, when the child believes all that is told him by his parents and teachers. He believes what he is taught to believe. At this stage ideas are external to him. He forms mental pictures of his religious objects, such as God, Jesus, the apostles, heaven, and so forth. He thinks in *percepts*. His religious objects are persons, things, places; and these are external to himself, entities apart from and beyond himself.

(2) Then comes the period of intellection, when the stage of *conceptual* thinking is reached. The child begins to reflect on the meaning of what he has come to believe. It is at this stage that intellectual problems and doubts arise. The youth has entered upon the stage of ideation.

(3) There then follows a process either of (a) *acceptance and personal committal*, when the subject internalises the ideas which hitherto have been external to him, and identifies himself personally with them; or (b) *rejection*, when the subject breaks away from, or rejects, the ideas he has been taught; or (c) *modification*, in which the subject selects from what he has learned in the past, adapts his earlier ideas to his own growing personal needs and experience, and creates the pattern of a new orientation.

It is this process of acceptance, or rejection, or modification that constitutes conversion. Here we see conversion in its true perspective. Here are all the elements of conditioning, response, and integration. If this is the kind of conversion the evangelist is seeking to stimulate, then he is justified in his efforts, for he is helping an individual "to come to himself". But if he is trying to foist his own religious ideas upon another, and seeking to press him through his own particular mould, he is undertaking a task that is fraught with difficulty and even danger.

There is another aspect of conversion in relation to personal religious experience, which ought to be considered. The convert himself must realise that the process of conversion is but the beginning of his spiritual pilgrimage. The religious sentiment must grow. Adolescence is the time when the majority of Christians begin to internalise their religious beliefs. Most conversions occur, or at least begin, in adolescence. The tragedy is that many Christians in adult life are content to live at an adolescent level: emotionally and intellectually their religious outlook is not that of a developed adult. It cannot be said too frequently, that conversion is but the beginning of the religious pilgrimage. Christian maturity involves emotional and intellectual, as well as ethical and mystical, advancement.

Conversion and the Work of the Church

If we accept this broad interpretation of conversion, if we see it as a personal response, with the individual freely accepting, or rejecting, or modifying the ideas and ideals that have been presented to him, then we see it as a normal part of the Church's work. There is no antipathy between the work of the pastor and that of the evangelist. Indeed, often the best evangelistic work can be done by the pastor who knows his people and can enter understandingly and sympathetically into their problems and needs. And if the pastor knows his people in their homes, so much the better; for the pastor who knows their home background is in a better position to help them than he would be if he knew them only in church.

The work of the pastor–evangelist is that of a physician of souls. Sometimes he will hear confessions. There is a cathartic value in confession. When an individual is in great distress he sometimes finds it helpful and relieving to unburden himself to another. This fact is recognised even by those who do not normally "hear confessions". It is doubtful whether there is a pastor or professional evangelist of experience who has not at some time heard confessions.

Sometimes the pastor will spend a great deal of time in

helping a single individual. A growing number of clergy and ministers are recognising the value of psycho-therapeutic methods in dealing with the religious problems of individuals. Sometimes spiritual problems are found to be due to faulty religious teaching in early childhood. In some cases the religious problem is co-existent with other and deeper psychological troubles. Sometimes it turns out to be not a religious problem at all. If the pastor is wise in handling such cases he may find it necessary to seek the help of a physician or an expert psychiatrist. Co-operation between pastor and physician can be a fruitful source of help in the service of suffering humanity. Some clergy and ministers specialise in this type of ministry, and although at the moment their number is small, their success is undoubted. Such a ministry calls for special training and, to some extent, for special gifts; but it is a rewarding ministry to any who undertake it.

Postscript

Much more could have been written on each of the topics touched upon in this book; but I have aimed at brevity. This is not intended to be in any sense a definitive work. It is offered as a humble contribution to an enormous and difficult subject. Perhaps sufficient has been said, however, to indicate the large range of topics and the wide field of research that are still open to serious pastors and teachers, and to all students of religious experience. There is still much more to be discovered, and much more to be said; but here by way of summary, let us reiterate our main findings:

(1) Religious conversion, in the sense of consciously turning from one attitude to religion to another, is by no means a universal experience amongst those who profess and call themselves Christians. For many — perhaps for the majority — of them, the religious life grows quietly and almost imperceptibly. If we must speak of conversion in their case

(for conversion is a matter of response), we have to call it unconscious conversion.

(2) When conversions do occur, the important factors are: The conditioning process; the personal response of the subject; and the integration of the convert's life with that of the group — in this case, the life of fellowship within the Church.

(3) When studying conversions, or when seeking pastorally to help someone in spiritual difficulties in relation to his conversion, it is necessary to give full consideration to both the internal states of the subject, and the external pressures imposed upon him, at the time of his conversion.

(4) When all these facts and factors are taken into account, it becomes clear that *conversion* must be given a wider connotation than it is sometimes accorded. Conversion may not always mean a guilt-conscious sinner seeking the forgiveness of a holy but loving Saviour. It may mean the following out of a great Ideal; or the discovery of the way of release from fear, from crippling inferiority-feeling, or from some other unhappy state of inner conflict. It may be a process of personal acceptance, rejection, or modification of ideas and ideals hitherto presented to the subject. Perhaps it could mean many other things if only the process were more clearly understood, and the basis of evangelistic appeal broadened.

(5) The question of what does constitute the message of evangelism is a matter which calls for urgent and enlightened discussion, with all possible theological knowledge, psychological insight, and practical experience to aid the discussion.

(6) Finally, when all the facts are considered, it seems reasonable to conclude that the best evangelistic work can be done by the parish priest or the resident minister, who is trained for the work and who has behind him all the spiritual

resources inherent in the life of the Church — in its fellowship, its worship, its sacraments, and its service.

The work of the pastor is a delicate and sacred one. He must make a personal — sometimes an intimate — approach to others; he comes face to face with human need and distress; he is often the last human support of those in sickness, bereavement, and of those who pass through the valley of the shadow of death; he shares the intimate confidences of those who seek his help; he hears their confessions; he grapples with their problems and with their intellectual doubts. This is no work for the novice or for those who have a theological axe to grind. It calls for knowledge and wisdom, for patience and understanding, and, above all, for the consecration of himself and all his powers to the service and well-being of those to whom he is sent.

BIBLIOGRAPHY

ALLPORT, G. W., *The Individual and His Religion: A Psychological Interpretation.* London: Constable & Co., 1951.

CITRON, B., *New Birth: A Study of the Evangelical Doctrine of Conversion in the Protestant Fathers.* Edinburgh: The University Press, 1951.

CLARK, WALTER H., *The Psychology of Religion: An Introduction to Religious Experience and Behaviour.* New York: The Macmillan Company, 1958.

COE, George A., *The Psychology of Religion.* Chicago: The University of Chicago Press, 1916.

COLQUHOUN, FRANK, *Harringay Story: The Official Record of the Billy Graham Greater London Crusade, 1954.* London: Hodder & Stoughton Ltd., 1955.

DE BLANK, JOOST, *This is Conversion.* London: Hodder & Stoughton Ltd., 1957.

GREEN, BRYAN, *The Practice of Evangelism.* London: Hodder & Stoughton Ltd., 1951.

JACKSON, GEORGE, *The Fact of Conversion.* London: Hodder & Stoughton Ltd., 1909.

JAMES, WILLIAM, *The Varieties of Religious Experience.* London: Longmans, Green & Co. Ltd., 1947 edition.

MASON, ARTHUR J., *The Ministry of Conversion.* London: Longmans, Green & Co. Ltd., 1906.

Methodism, the Message and Mission of: Report of Methodist Conference Committee, 1943. London: Epworth Press, 1946.

NEILL, STEPHEN C., "Conversion," *Scottish Journal of Theology,* Vol. 3, No. 4, December, 1950.

NOCK, A. D., *Conversion: The Old and the New in Religion from Alexander the Great to Augustine of Hippo.* Oxford: Clarendon Press, 1933.

NORTHRIDGE, W. L., *Recent Psychology and Evangelistic Preaching.* London: Epworth Press, 1924.

PRATT, J. B., *The Religious Consciousness: A Psychological Study.* New York: The Macmillan Company, 1941.

ROUTLEY, ERIK, *The Gift of Conversion.* London: Lutterworth Press, 1957.

SARGANT, WILLIAM, *Battle for the Mind: A Physiology of Conversion and Brain-Washing.* London: Heinemann, 1957.

STARBUCK, E. D., *The Psychology of Religion: An Empirical Study of the Growth of Religious Consciousness.* London: Walter Scott, 1901.

Towards the Conversion of England: Report of the Archbishops' Committee, 1945. Press and Publications Board of the Church Assembly, 1945.

UNDERWOOD, A. C., *Conversion: Christian and Non-Christian. A Comparative and Psychological Study.* London: George Allen and Unwin, Ltd., 1925.

WALKER, ALAN, *The Whole Gospel for the Whole World.* London: Marshall, Morgan & Scott, 1958.

WARREN, MAX, *Interpreters: A Study in Contemporary Evangelism.* London: Highway Press, 1936.

WATERHOUSE, ERIC S., *Psychology and Pastoral Work.* London: University of London Press, 1939.

WEBSTER, DOUGLAS, *What is Evangelism?* London: Highway Press, 1959.

WEDEL, THEODORE O., "Evangelism an Essay in Criticism," *The Ecumenical Review*, Vol. III, No. 4, July, 1951.

WEDEL, THEODORE O., "Evangelism's Threefold Witness: Kerygma, Koinonia, Diakonia," *The Ecumenical Review*, Vol. IX, No. 3, April, 1957.

YEAXLEE, BASIL A., *Religion and the Growing Mind.* London: Nisbet & Co., 1945.